GRAMMY, GRAMMY Awards and the gramophone logo are registered
trademarks of The Recording Academy® and are used under license.

Visit The Recording Academy Online at
www.grammy.com

ISBN 978-1-4584-1561-5

HAL•LEONARD®
CORPORATION

7777 W. BLUEMOUND RD. P.O. BOX 13819 MILWAUKEE, WI 53213

Visit Hal Leonard Online at
www.halleonard.com

>> Adele at the 54th GRAMMY Awards

THE RECORDING ACADEMY®

When it comes to music on TV, the last few years alone have seen some very memorable moments: Paul McCartney, Bruce Springsteen, Dave Grohl, and Joe Walsh jamming on "The End" from the Beatles' classic *Abbey Road*; Adele making her triumphant first live singing appearance after throat surgery to perform "Rolling In The Deep"; Pink dripping wet and hovering 20 feet above the stage while singing a note-perfect version of "Glitter In The Air"; and Lady Gaga hatching from a massive egg to perform "Born This Way." All of these performances, and many more, took place on the famed GRAMMY Awards® stage.

The GRAMMY® Award is indisputedly the most sought-after recognition of excellence in recorded music worldwide. Over more than half a century, the GRAMMY Awards have become both music's biggest honor and Music's Biggest Night®, with the annual telecast drawing tens of millions of viewers nationwide and millions more internationally.

And with evolving categories that always reflect important current artistic waves — such as dance/electronica music — as well as setting a record for social TV engagement in 2012, the GRAMMYs keep moving forward, serving as a real-time barometer of music's cultural impact.

The Recording Academy is the organization that produces the GRAMMY Awards. Consisting of the artists, musicians, songwriters, producers, engineers, and other professionals who make the music you enjoy every day on the radio, your streaming or download services, or in the concert hall, The Academy is a dynamic institution with an active agenda aimed at supporting and nurturing music and the people who make it.

Whether it's joining with recording artists to ensure their creative rights are protected, providing ongoing professional development services to the recording community or supporting the health and well-being of music creators and music education in our schools, The Recording Academy has become the recording industry's primary organization for professional and educational outreach, human services, arts advocacy, and cultural enrichment.

The Academy represents members from all corners of the professional music world — from the biggest recording stars to unsung music educators — all brought together under the banner of building a better creative environment for music and its makers.

>> Paul McCartney at the 2012 MusiCares Person of the Year gala in his honor

>> Trombone Shorty and Mavis Staples at the GRAMMY Foundation's Music Preservation Project event in 2012

MUSICARES FOUNDATION®

MusiCares® was established by The Recording Academy to provide a safety net of critical assistance for music people in times of need. MusiCares has developed into a premier support system for music people, providing resources to cover a wide range of financial, medical and personal emergencies through innovative programs and services, including regular eBay auctions of one-of-a-kind memorabilia that are open to the public. The charity has been supported by the contributions and participation of artists such as Neil Diamond, Aretha Franklin, Paul McCartney, Bruce Springsteen, Barbra Streisand, and Neil Young — just to name the organization's most recent annual Person of the Year fundraiser honorees — and so many others through the years.

THE GRAMMY FOUNDATION®

The GRAMMY Foundation's mission is to cultivate the understanding, appreciation and advancement of the contribution of recorded music to American culture. The Foundation accomplishes this mission through programs and activities designed to engage the music industry and cultural community as well as the general public. The Foundation works to bring national attention to important issues such as the value and impact of music and arts education and the urgency of preserving our rich cultural legacy, and it accomplishes this work by engaging music professionals — from big-name stars to working professionals and educators — to work directly with students.

>> Secretary of the Department of Health and Human Services Kathleen Sebelius and Recording Academy President/CEO Neil Portnow present the Recording Artists' Coalition Award to John Mayer at the GRAMMYs on the Hill Awards in Washington, D.C., in 2012

Paul Morigi/WireImage.com

>> The GRAMMY Museum in downtown Los Angeles

Courtesy of the GRAMMY Museum

FIGHTING FOR MUSICIANS' RIGHTS

Over the last 15 years, The Recording Academy has built a presence in the nation's capital, working to amplify the voice of music creators in national policy matters. Today, called the "supersized musicians lobby" by *Congressional Quarterly*, The Academy's Advocacy & Industry Relations office in Washington, D.C., is the leading representative of the collective world of recording professionals — artists, songwriters, producers, and engineers — through its GRAMMYs on the Hill® Initiative. The Academy has taken a leadership role in the fight to expand radio performance royalties to all music creators, worked on behalf of musicians on censorship concerns and regularly supported musicians on legislative issues that impact the vitality of music.

THE GRAMMY MUSEUM®

Since opening its doors in December 2008, the GRAMMY Museum has served as a dynamic educational and interactive institution dedicated to the power of music. The four-story, 30,000-square foot facility is part of L.A. Live, the premier sports and entertainment destination in downtown Los Angeles. The Museum serves the community with interactive, permanent and traveling exhibits and an array of public and education programs. We invite you to visit us when you're in the Los Angeles area.

As you can see, The Recording Academy is so much more than the annual GRAMMY telecast once a year, even if that one show is Music's Biggest Night. To keep up with all The Academy's activities, visit GRAMMY.com regularly, and join the conversation on our social networks:

Facebook.com/TheGRAMMYs

Twitter.com/TheGRAMMYs

YouTube.com/TheGRAMMYs

TheGRAMMYs.tumblr.com

Foursquare.com/TheGRAMMYs

Instagram (user name: TheGRAMMYs)

Google+ (gplus.to/TheGRAMMYs)

TABLE OF CONTENTS (ALPHABETICAL)

TABLE OF CONTENTS (CHRONOLOGICAL)

AMERICAN BOY

Words and Music by KANYE WEST, KEITH HARRIS,
ESTELLE SWARAY, WILL ADAMS, JOHN STEPHENS,
CALEB SPEIR, JOSH LOPEZ and KWELI WASHINGTON

Moderate groove

Rap 1: *(See rap lyrics)*

Take me on a trip, __ I'd like to go __ some - day. __

Take me to New York, __ I'd love to see __ L. __ A. __ I real - ly want to __ come

kick it with you. __ You'll be my A - mer - i - can __ boy. __

Emaj7   Cmaj7

He said, "Hey sis - ta', _____ it's real - ly, real - ly nice to meet _____
- end? _____ Take me _____ to Broad - way. _____

Am7   Dm9

_____ ya." _____ I _____ just met _____ this five - foot - sev - en guy who's just _____ my type. _____
_____ Let's _____ go shop - pin', may - be then _____ we'll go to a _____ ca - fé. _____

Emaj7   Cmaj7

_____ I like the way _____ he's speak - in', _____ his con - fi - dence _____ is peak -
_____ Let's go on _____ the sub - way, _____ take me to _____ your hood.

Am7   Fmaj7

- in'. _____ Don't like _____ his bag - gy jeans, _____ but I'm - a like _____ what's un - der - neath _____
_____ I nev - er been _____ to Brook - lyn and _____ I'd like _____ to see _____ what's good. _____

Emaj7 / **Cmaj7**

them.___ And, no, I ain't been to M - I - A._____ I
Dressed in _____ all your fan - cy clothes, _____

Am7 / **Dm9**

heard that Cal - i nev - er rains __ and New _ York's all __ the way. _
sneak - ers look - in' fresh _ to death. _ I'm lov - in' those _ shell toes. _

Emaj7 / **Cmaj7**

First, let's see the West _ End, _____ I'll show you to my bed - room. _____ I'm
Walk - in' _____ that _ walk, _____ talk that _____ slick _ talk. ____

N.C.

lik - in' this A - mer - i - can ___ boy, _____ A - mer - i - can boy.

Take me on a trip, I'd like to go someday. Take me to New York, I'd love to
see L. A. I really want to come kick it with you.
You'll be my American boy, American boy. La, la, la,
la, la. La, la, la, la, la. La, la, la,

la, la. _____ Will you be my A - mer - i - can _____ boy, ___

D.S. al Coda

_____ A - mer - i - can boy? _____ Can we get a - way this week -

CODA

You'll be my A - mer - i - can _____ boy. ___

Rap 2: *(See rap lyrics)*

And you thought __ he was cute be-fore, look at this pea-coat. Tell me he's broke.

Would you be my ___ love, my ___ love? Would you be my ___

___ love, my ___ love? Could you be my ___ love, my ___ love? Would

you be my A - mer - i - can ___ boy, ___ A - mer - i - can boy?

Take me on a trip, _ I'd like to go _ some - day. _

{ Take me to Chi - ca - go, San Fran-
{ Take me to New York, _ I'd love to

cis - co Bay. _ }
see _ L. _ A. _ }   I real - ly want to ___ come kick it with you. _

You'll be my A - mer - i - can _ boy, _____ A - mer - i - can boy.

La, la, la, _____ la, la. _____ La, la, la, _

Additional Lyrics

Rap 1: Just a number one champion sound. Yeah, Estelle, we 'bout to get down.
Who the hottest in the world right now? Just touched down in London town.
Bet they give me a pound. Put the money in my hand right now.
Tell the promoter we need more seats. We just sold out all the floor seats.

Rap 2: Who's killin' 'em in th U.K. Everybody gonna say, "You K."
Reluctantly, 'cause most of this press don't fuck wit' me.
Estelle once said to me, "Cool down, down. Don't act a fool now, now."
I always act a fool, ow, ow. Ain't nothin' new now, now.
He crazy, I know what you're thinkin'. Rappin', I know what you're drinkin'.
Rap singer, chain blinger. Holla at the next chick soon as you're blinkin'.
What's your persona about this Americana rhymer? Am I shallow 'cause all my clothes designer?
Dress smart like a London bloke. Before he speak, his suit bespoke.
And you thought he was cute before. Look at this peacoat, tell me he's broke.
And I know you ain't into all that. I heard your lyrics, I feel your spirit.
But I still talk that ca, a, ash 'cause a lotta wag's wanna hear it.
And I'm feelin' like Mike at his baddest, like the Pips at their Gladys.
And I know they love it so to hell wit' all that rubbish.

BE WITHOUT YOU

Words and Music by MARY J. BLIGE,
JOHNTA AUSTIN, BRYAN MICHAEL COX
and JASON PERRY

Moderate groove

I wan-na be with you, got-ta be with you, need to be with you.

Oh, _____ oh, _____ I wan-na be with you, got-ta be with you, need to be with you.

Oh, _____ oh, _____ ooh, _____

oh, _____ oh, _____ ooh. _____

Chem-is-try was cra-zy from the get go. Nei-ther one of us knew why. _

We did-n't deal noth-in' o-ver-night 'cause a love like this _ takes some time. _

Peo-ple swore it off as a phase, said _ we can't see that. Now

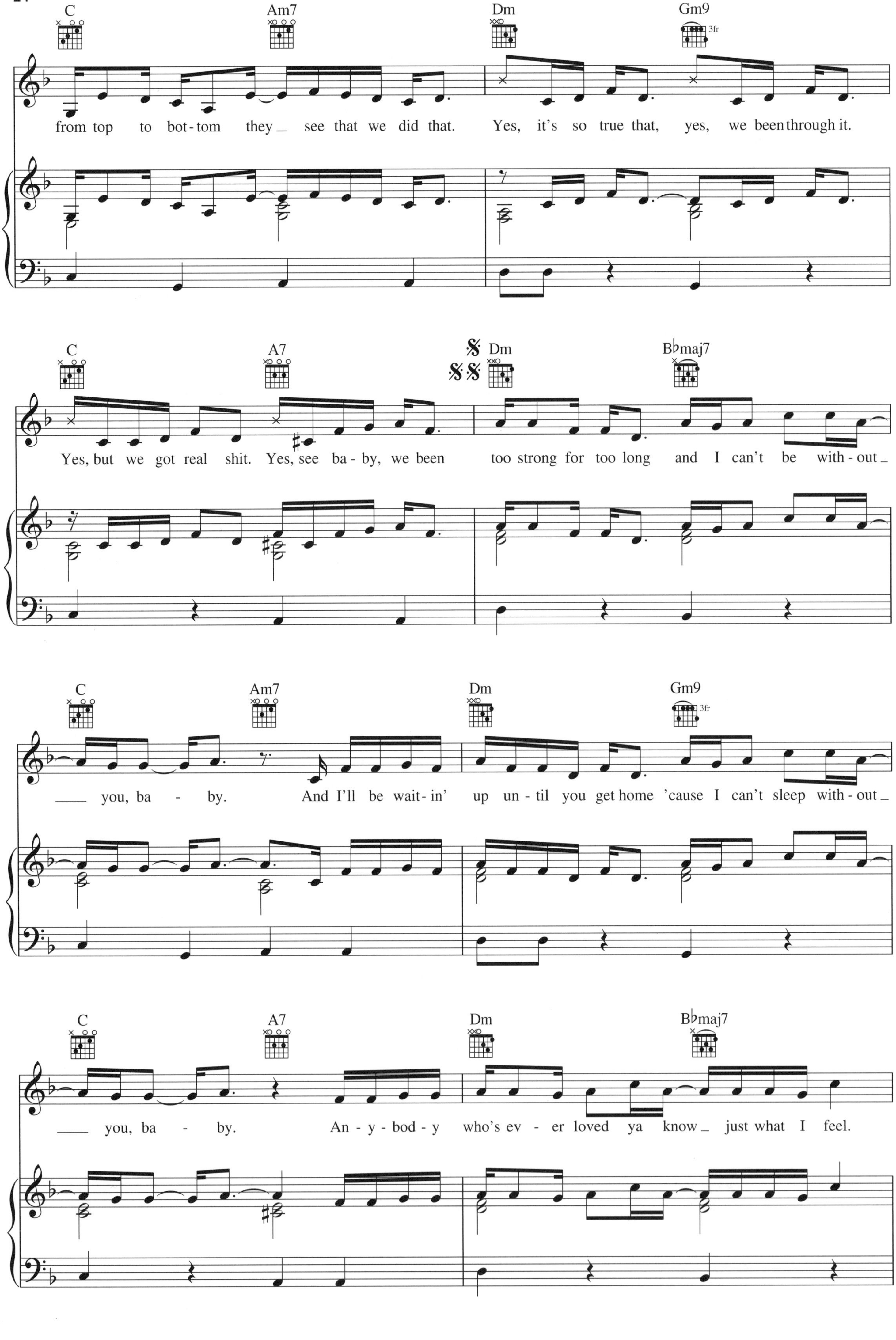

C   Am7   Dm   Gm9

Too hard to fake it. Noth-in' can re-place it. Call the ra-di-o if you __ just can't be with-out __

C   A7   **To Coda I** 🔶 Dm   B♭maj7

To Coda II 🔶🔶

__ your ba - by.   I got a ques-tion for ya, see I al-read-y know the

C   Am7   Dm   Gm9

an - swer. _____ Still __ I wan-na ask you, would you lie? No. __ Make me cry? No. __ Do some-

C   A7   Dm   B♭maj7

thin' be-hind my back and then try __ cov-er it up? Well, nei-ther would I, _____ ba -

C   Am7   Dm   Gm9

-by. My love is on-ly ev-'ry love. Yes, I'll be faith-ful. Yes, love for real.

C   A7   **D.S. al Coda I**

Yes, and with us you'll al-ways ___ know the deal. We been

CODA I   Gm7   Am7   B♭maj7   Am7

See this is real talk, I'm 'a al-ways stay _____ no mat-ter what. Through the

Gm7   Am7   B♭maj7   A7

bad, ___ thick and thin, right or wrong. ___ All day ev-'ry day. _____ Now, if you're

Dm · **N.C.**

down_ on_ love or don't be-lieve_ this ain't for you. No,_ this_ ain't for you.
And if you got it

deep in your heart, _ and deep down you know _ that it's true,___ well, let me see ya' put your
Come on, _ come on, ____ come on. _

Dm · **Bbmaj7** · **C** · **Am7**

hands_ up, hands up. Fel-las, tell your la-dy she's the one.____ Oh, put your

Dm · **Gm9** · **C** · **A7**

D.S.S. al Coda II

hands_ up, hands up. La-dies, let him know he's got your love. _
Look him right in his eyes _ and tell _ him. We been

CODA II

I wan-na be with you, got-ta be with you, need to be with you.

I wan-na be with you, got-ta be with you, need to be with you.

Optional Ending

Repeat and Fade

BEAUTIFUL

Words and Music by
LINDA PERRY

Moderately slow

Whispered: Don't look at me.

Ev-'ry day ___ is so
To all your friends ___ you're de-

Eb/Db   Cm   B(b5)

won-der-ful,   then sud-den-ly, ____   it's hard to breathe. _
lir-i-ous.   So con-sumed _   in all your doom. ___

Eb   Eb/Db

Now and then ___   I get in-se-cure ___   from all the pain, _
Try-ing hard ___   to fill the emp-ti-ness. _   The piec-es gone, _

Cm   B(b5)

___   feel so a-shamed. _
___   left the puz-zle un-done. ___ Ain't that the way it is? ___

Ab   Fm

I am beau-ti-ful _____   no mat-ter what _ they say. __
You are beau-ti-ful _____   no mat-ter what _ they say. __
'Cause we are beau-ti-ful _____   no mat-ter what _ they say. __

So don't you __ bring me down to-day. _____ No mat-ter what __ we do. __

__ No mat-ter what __ we say. __ We're the song in-side __ the tune __

__ full of beau-ti-ful mis-takes. And ev-'ry-where __ we go __

__ the sun will al-ways shine. __ And to-mor-row we might a-wake __ on ___ the oth - er side.

D.S. al Coda
(Take 1st ending)

CODA

to - day. ___

Don't you bring me down ___

to - day, ___ yeah, ___ ooh. ___

Don't you bring me down ___ um ___ to - day.

BEAUTIFUL DAY

Lyrics by BONO
Music by U2

Moderately

The heart is a bloom, _____ shoots up through the ston-y ground. _____ But there's no room, _____

It's a beautiful day.

Verse 1: to take you out of this place. Some-one you could lend a hand in return for grace. It's a beau-ti-ful day.

Verse 2: e-ven if that does-n't ring true. You've been all o-ver and it's been all o-ver you. It's a beau-ti-ful day. (2., D.S.) Don't

The sky falls. And you feel like it's a beau-ti-ful day.

let it get a-way. A beau-ti-ful day.

Chords: G, D(add9), D, A, E7sus/B, D, G, D(add9), D, A, A, Bm7, D, G(add9), G, D, A, Bm7, D

Don't let it get _ a - way. _____ You're on the road _____

Touch _____ me,

take me to _____ that oth - er _____ place.

Teach me, _____
Reach me, _____

I know I'm not a hope - less _____ case.

See the world in green and blue. __

See Chi - na right ____ in front of you. See the can - yons

bro - ken by cloud. See the tu - na fleets clear - ing the ___ sea out.

BEFORE HE CHEATS

Words and Music by JOSH KEAR
and CHRIS TOMPKINS

Steady Country Swing-Rock

Right now, he's prob-'ly slow danc-ing with a bleach-blonde tramp and she's
Right now, she's prob-'ly up sing-ing some white trash ver-sion of Sha-

prob-'ly get-ting frisk-y. Right now, he's prob-'ly buy-ing her some
ni - a ka-ra-o-ke. Right now, she's prob-'ly say-ing, "I'm drunk"

carved my name in - to his leath-er seat. _____ I took a

Lou-is-ville Slug-ger to both ___ head - lights, _ slashed a hole _ in all ___ four tires, _ and

To Coda ⊕

may-be next time _ he'll think _____ be - fore _ he _____ cheats.

_____ be - fore _ he _____ cheats. _____

BLESS THE BROKEN ROAD

Words and Music by MARCUS HUMMON,
BOBBY BOYD and JEFF HANNA

Moderately

I set out on a nar-row way man-y years a-go,

hop-ing I would find true love a-long the bro-ken road. But

I got lost _ a time _ or _ two, _ wiped my brow _ and kept push-in' through. _

I could-n't see _ how ev-er-y sign _ point-ed straight _ to you. _

But ev-er-y _ long lost _ dream _ led me to where you _ are. _

_ Oth-ers who broke my _ heart, _ they were like north-ern stars _ point-ing me on my _____ way _____ in - to your lov - ing _____ arms. _____

This much I know _____ is _____ true: that

God blessed _____ the bro - ken road _____ that led me straight _____ to you. _____

Yes, He did. _____

D.S. al Coda

er plan ___ that is com - in' true. ___ Ev - er - y

CODA N.C.

Now I'm just a - roll - in' ___ home ___

in-to my lov - er's _____ arms. _____ This much I
know _____ is _____ true: that God blessed _ the bro -
- ken road _____ that led me straight _____ to you, _____
that God blessed _ the bro -

-ken road _____ that led me straight ___

to you.

BREATHE

Words and Music by HOLLY LAMAR
and STEPHANIE BENTLEY

Moderately fast

I can feel the mag - ic float - ing in the air.

Be - ing with you gets me that

way.

I watch the sun-

-light dance a - cross ___ your face ___ and I ___

nev - er been this swept a - way. ___

All my thoughts just seem to set - tle on ___ the breeze ___
In a way I know my heart ___ is wak - ing up ___

Am7(add4)   **G/B**   **C**

when I'm ly - in' wrapped _ up in ___ your arms.
as ___ all the walls ___ come tum - bling down.

C(add9)   **Am7**   **G/B**

The whole world just fades a - way, ___ the on -
Clos - er than just I've ev - er felt ___ be - fore, _

C   **G/B**   **Am7**

- ly thing ___ I hear is the
___ and I know ___ and you know there's no

Dsus   **D**

beat - ing of ___ your heart. ___
need for words right now. ___

'Cause I can feel you

G

breathe, it's wash-ing o - ver me, and sud - den - ly I'm melt - ing in - to you.

D **G** **Am7**

There's noth-ing left to prove, ba - by, all we need is just __ to be __

C **D** **G**

caught __ up in the touch, the slow and stead - y

Am7 **C** **G/B** **Am7**

rush. Ba - by, is - n't that the way __ that love's __ sup - posed _____ to be?

I can feel you breathe.

Just breathe.

Caught up in the

CHASING PAVEMENTS

Words and Music by ADELE ADKINS
and FRANCIS EG WHITE

Moderate R&B

Lyrics:

I've made up my mind, ___ don't need to think it o-ver; if I'm wrong I am right, ___ don't need to look no fur-ther. This ain't lust. I ___ know this is love.

To Coda

D.S. al Coda

if I knew my place? Should I leave it there? _ Should I give up _ or should I

just keep chas - in' pave - ments _ e - ven if it leads no - where? _____ Ooh. _____ I

build my - self up _____ and fly a - round in cir - cles, wait then as my heart drops _ and my

back be - gins to tin - gle. Fi - nal - ly, could _____ this be it? Or

Lyrics:

pave-ments? _ Oh. ___ Should I give up ___ or should I just keep chas-in' pave-ments _

e-ven if it leads no-where? ____ Or would it be a waste e-ven

if I knew my place? Should I leave it there? __ Should I give up ___ or should I

just keep chas-in' pave-ments _ e-ven if it leads no-where? _____ Ooh. _____

DANCE WITH MY FATHER

Words by LUTHER VANDROSS
and RICHARD MARX
Music by LUTHER VANDROSS

Moderately slow

Back when I was a child, be-fore life re-moved all the in-no-cence, my fa-ther would lift me high and dance with my moth-

Lyrics:

-er and me ___ and then ___ spin me a-round till I fell ___

___ a-sleep, ___ then up the stairs he would car-

-ry me. ___ And I knew ___ for sure ___ I was loved. ___

If I could get ___ an-oth-er chance, ___ an-
I could steal ___ one fi-nal glance, ___ one ___

Gm · Eb · Cm

oth - er walk, __ an - oth - er dance __ with him,
fi - nal step, __ one fi - nal dance __ with him,

I'd play a song that would nev -

Gm · Eb

- er, ev - er end.

How I'd love, __ love, love _____ to
'Cause I'd love, __ love, love _____ to

Fsus · F · **To Coda** ⊕ Bb · F/A

dance with my fa - ther a - gain. ____
dance with my fa - ther a - gain. __

Gm · Eb · Bb

When I and my moth - er __ would dis -

- a - gree, to get my way I would run ____ from her ___ to him. ___

He'd make me laugh just __ to com - fort me, yeah, yeah, ___ then fi - nal - ly make me do __

___ just what my ma - ma said. _____ Lat - er that night when I was ___

___ a - sleep, _ he left a dol - lar un - der _____ my sheet. _ Nev - er dreamed _

C/E   Cm   Fsus   F

D.S. al Coda

_____ that he _____ would be gone _____ from me. _____ If

CODA

B♭   E♭   F

_____ Some-times I'd lis - ten out - side _____ her door _____

B♭   F/A   Gm

and I'd hear how my moth - er cried _____ for him. _____

E♭   Fsus   F   Cm7

I pray for her e - ven more _____ than me.   I pray for her e - ven more _____

Fsus   F   Fsus2   B♭

___ than me. _____

F/A   Gm9   E♭(add9)

I

C   G/B   Am9

know I'm pray-ing for much too much, _ but _ could you send _ back the

F   Dm7   Am9

on-ly man _ she loved? I know you don't do it u-su-al-ly _____ but, dear _ Lord, _

COMPLICATED

Words and Music by AVRIL LAVIGNE, LAUREN CHRISTY,
SCOTT SPOCK and GRAHAM EDWARDS

Uh huh, uh huh, that's the way it is.

Chill out, what-cha yell - in' for? Lay back, it's all been done __ be - fore.
You came o - ver un - an - nounced, dressed up like you're some - thing else.

And if you could on - ly __ let it be __ you will see. __
Where you are ain't where __ it's __ at, you see. __ You're mak - in' me __

I like you the way __ you are when we're driv - in' in __ your car
laugh out when you strike __ your pose. Take off all your prep - py clothes.
Lay back, it's all been done __ be - fore.

Bb(add9) | **C**

and you're talk-in' to ___ me one on one ___ but you be-come ___
You know you're not fool-in' an-y-one ___ when you be-come ___
And if you could on-ly let it be ___ you will see ___

Bb(add9) | **Dm** | **To Coda** ⊕

some-bod-y else 'round ev-'ry-one else. You're watch-ing your back like you can't re-lax. ___ You're

Bb(add9) | **C5**

try'n' to be cool. You look like a fool to me. ___ Tell ___ me,

D5 | **Bb5** | **F5** | **C5**

why'd you have to go and make things so com-pli-cat-ed? See the way you're act-ing like you're some-bod-y else, __ gets me frus-trat - ed. __ Life's like this, you,

you fall __ and you crawl __ and you break __ and you take __ what you get __ and you turn __ it in - to

hon-es-ty and prom-ise me I'm nev-er gon-na find you fake __ it, _____ no, no,

no.   no,   no,   no,   no,

no, no, no, no, no, no, no, no,

no, no, no, no. Chill out, what - cha yell - in' for?

D.S. al Coda

CODA

try'n' to be cool. You look like a fool to me. _____ Tell me _____

why'd you have to go and make things so com - pli - cat - ed? See the way you're act-ing like you're some-bod-y else, __ gets me frus-trat - ed. __ Life's like this, you,

you fall __ and you crawl __ and you break __ and you take __ what you get __ and you turn __ it in - to

hon - es - ty. Prom-ise me I'm nev - er gon - na find you fake __ it, __ no, no,

__ it, __ no, no, __ no.

DEVILS & DUST

Words and Music by
BRUCE SPRINGSTEEN

Tune gtr. in Double Drop D:
⑥ = D   ③ = G
⑤ = A   ② = B
④ = D   ① = D

Moderately ♩ = 112

℅ *Verses 1-4:*

1. I've got my fin-ger on the trig - ger,
   home, Bob - bie,
   3. 4. *See additional lyrics*

but   I don't know who to trust.__
home's a long, long way from us.__

When I look in - to your eyes,__
Feel a dirt - y wind blow - in',__

there's just dev-ils and_____ dust.
dev-ils and_____ dust.

2.We're a long,___ long way from

Chorus:

{ I've got___ God on my }
{ We've got___ God on our }

side,_____ and { I'm } { we're } just try - ing to sur -

vive.___ What if what you do to sur - vive___ kills___ the things you

love? Fear's_ a pow - er-ful thing,___ it___ can turn your heart black, you can trust.___

dust.

(Harmonica solo ad lib....

Verses 5 & 6:

1.

2.

5. Now ev - 'ry wom-an and ev - 'ry_____ man,
...end solo)   ger,

D(4)   **G/D**

they wan - na take___ a right - eous stand,
and to - night, faith___ just ain't e - nough.

find the love___ that God___ wills___
When I look___ in - side___ my

D(4)   **Dsus**   **A7**   **D(4)**   **Dsus**

heart,

and the faith___ that he com - mands.
there's just dev - ils and dust.

|1.   **|2.**   *Chorus:*

D(4)   **Dsus**   **D(4)**   **Dsus**   **G**

6. I've got my fin - ger on the trig -   Well, I've got___ God on my side,___

D/F#

and I'm just try - ing to sur - vive.___   What if what you do to sur -

dust.

(Harmonica solo ad lib....)

Verse 3:
Well, I dreamed of you last night
In a field of blood and stone.
The blood began to dry,
And the smell began to rise.

Verse 4:
Well, I dreamed of you last night, Bob,
In a field of mud and bone.
Your blood began to dry
And the smell began to rise.
(To Chorus:)

DROPS OF JUPITER
(Tell Me)

Words and Music by PAT MONAHAN,
JIMMY STAFFORD, ROB HOTCHKISS,
CHARLIE COLIN and SCOTT UNDERWOOD

Moderately

Now that _____ she's back _____ in the at-
_____ she's back _____ from that soul _____

-mos- phere _____ with drops _____ of Ju- pi- ter in _____ her hair _____ hey
_____ va- ca- tion, trac- ing her way _____ through the con- stel- la- tion,

hey, _____
hey _____ hey. _____

she acts ____ like sum - mer and walks ___ like rain, ___ re - minds ___
She checks ___ out Mo - zart while she does Tae - Bo, ___ re - minds ___

___ me that ___ there's a time to change, ___ hey hey. _____
___ me that ___ there's ___ room to grow, ___ hey hey. _____

Since ___
Now that ___

C

_____ the re - turn _____ from her stay _____ on the moon, _____ she lis - tens like spring _____ and she talks _____
_____ she's back _____ in the at - mos - phere _____ I'm a - fraid _____ that she _____ might think

G

_____ like June. _____ Hey, hey, _____ plain old Jane, told a sto - ry 'bout a man who was
of me as _____

F

hey. _____
too a - fraid to fly so he nev - er did land. (1.,D.S.) But tell me, did you
(2.) But tell me, did the

G

sail a - cross _____ the sun? _____ Did you make it to the Milk - y _____ Way _____
wind sweep you off your feet? _____ Did you fin - 'lly get the chance to dance _____

G/A   **D**   **C/E**

to see ___ that lights ___ all fad - ed ___ and that heav - en is o -
a - long ___ the light ___ of day, ___ and head back to the

- ver - rat - ed? ___ And Tell me, did you fall for a shoot - ing star, ___
Milk - y Way? And tell me, did Ve - nus blow ___ your mind? ___

one ___ with - out a per - ma - nent scar? And did ___ you miss ___
Was it ev - 'ry - thing you want - ed to find and did ___ you miss ___

To Coda ⊕

me ___ while ___ you were look - ing for ___ your - self ___ out there?
me ___ while ___ you were look - ing for ___ your - self ___ out there?

Now that ___

90

Can you i-mag-ine no love, pride, _ deep - fried chick - en? Your

best friend _ al - ways stick - ing up for you, _

e - ven when I know you're wrong? _ Can you i - mag - ine no

first dance? _ Freeze - dried ro - mance? Five - hour _ phone con - ver - sa - tion? The best soy lat - te that you ev - er had ___ and

me? But tell me, did the

wind sweep you off your feet? ___ Did you fin - 'lly get the chance to dance ___

___ a - long ___ the light of day ___ and head back toward the

D.S. al Coda
Milk - y Way? And
CODA
C
self? Na na na
G
na na na na na na na na na na
F(add2)
na na na na. And did you fin - 'lly get the chance to dance a - long the light
C
of day? Na na na na na na

na na na na na na na na na na. And did you fall from a

shoot - ing star, fall from a shoot - ing star?

Na na na na na na na na na

na na na. And are you lone - ly look - ing for your - self out there?

rall.

DON'T KNOW WHY

Words and Music by
JESSE HARRIS

I don't know why ____ I did-n't come, ____ I ____ don't know why I did-n't come.

When I saw ____ the break ___ of day, ____

I wished that I ____ could fly ___ a - way ___ 'stead of kneel - ing in the sand ___ catch - ing tear - drops in my __ hand. __ My heart is __ drenched __ in __ wine, __

__ but you'll be __ on __

__ my __ mind __ for - ev - er. __

Out a - cross __ the end - less sea, __ I would die __ in ec-

Lyrics: er. ... Some - thing has ___ to ___ make ___ you run. ___

FALLIN'

Words and Music by
ALICIA KEYS

Freely

N.C.

I keep on fall-in' in _____ (Vocal ad lib.) and

Moderate Blues tempo

Em | Bm7 | Em | Bm7

out of love with-a you. Some-times _ I

Em | Bm7 | Em | Bm7

love you some-times you make me blue. Some-times I feel

I _____ nev - er felt this a

way. _____ How do you give me so much

pleas - ure and cause me so much pain? _____ Yeah, ___ yeah. _ Just when I

think _____ I'm tak-ing more than would a fool, _____ I ___ start

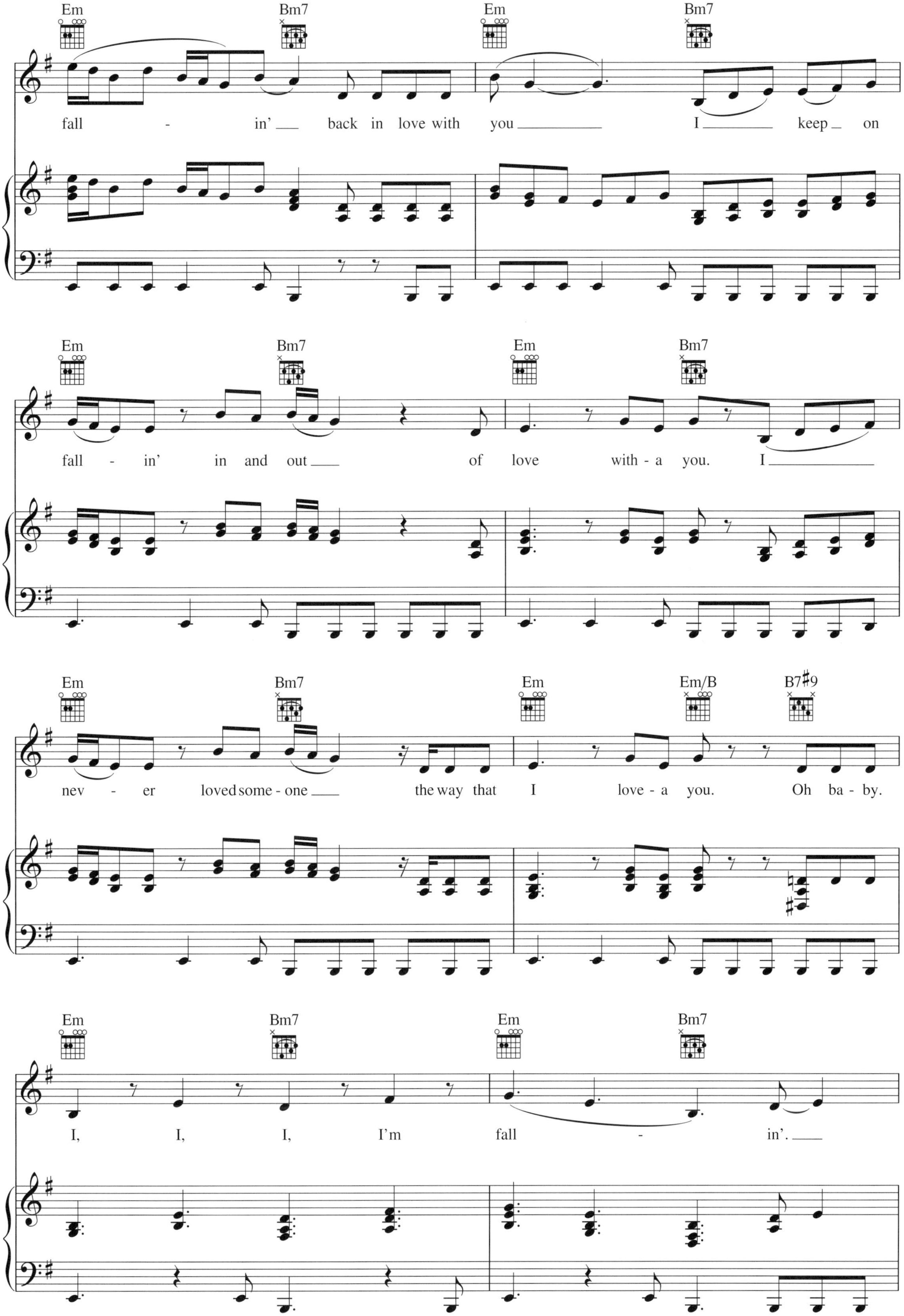

love with - a you. I _____ nev - er loved some - one _____ the way that

I love - a you. I'm _____ fall - in' in and out _____ of

love with - a you. I _____ nev - er loved some - one _____ the way that

I love - a you. I'm _____ fall - in' in and out _____ of

love with-a you. I _____ nev - er loved some - one ___ the way that

I love-a you. What?

HEY THERE DELILAH

Words and Music by
TOM HIGGENSON

Moderately

Hey there, De-li-lah, what's _ it like in New _ York Cit - y? I'm a thou -
Hey there, De-li-lah, I _____ know times are get - ting hard, but just be - lieve _

- sand miles a - way, _ but, girl, _ to - night _ you look so pret - ty, yes, you do.
___ me, girl, some-day _ I'll pay _ the bills _ with this gui - tar, we'll have it good.

Times Square can't shine as bright as you. ___ I swear it's true.
We'll have the life we knew we would. _ My word is good.

Hey there, De - li - lah, don't_ you wor - ry a - bout the dis - tance, I'm right
Hey there, De - li - lah, I've _ got so _ much left to say. _ If ev - 'ry

there. If you get lone - ly, give _ this song an - oth - er lis - ten. Close your eyes. _
sim - ple song I wrote _ to you _ would take your breath a - way, _ I'd write it all. ___

___
___ Lis - ten to my voice, it's my dis - guise. _
E - ven more in love _ with me, _ you'd

G
A
thou-sand miles seems pret-ty far, but they've got planes and trains and cars. I'd walk
D5
D5/A
Bm
Bm/A
to you if I had no oth-er way. Our
G
A
friends would all make fun of us, and we'll just laugh a-long be-cause we know
D5
D5/C♯
Bm
Bm/A
that none of them have felt this way. De-

G   A

li - lah, I can prom - ise you __ that by __ the time __ we __ get through, __ the world __

Bm

__ will nev - er, ev - er be the same, _____ and you're to blame. __

A

D5   F#m

Hey there, De - li - lah, you be good __ and don't you miss __ me. Two more

I HOPE YOU DANCE

Words and Music by TIA SILLERS
and MARK D. SANDERS

hope you nev - er lose _____ your sense of won - der.
nev - er fear _____ those _____ moun - tains in the dis - tance.

Gm7

You get your fill _____ to eat, _____ but al - ways keep that
Nev - er set - tle for _____ the path _____ of least re -

hun - ger. May you nev - er take _____ one
sist - ance. Liv - in' might mean tak - in'

E♭

sin - gle breath _____ for grant - ed. God for - bid _____
chanc - es, but they're worth tak - in'. Lov - in' might _____

F

_____ love ev - er leave _____ you emp - ty - hand - ed.
_____ be a mis - take, _____ but it's _____ worth mak - in'.

%. Eᵇ   F

I hope you still ____ feel small ____ when you stand be - side ____ the
Don't let ____ some hell - bent ____ heart leave ____ you

Bᵇ   Eᵇ   F

o - cean. When - ev - er one ____ door clos - es, I ____
bit - ter. When you come close ____ to sell - in' out, ____

Bᵇ

____ hope one ____ more o - pens. Prom - ise me ____
____ re - con - sid - er. Give the heav -

Cm7   Bᵇ/D

____ that you'll ____ give faith ____ a fight - ing
- ens a - bove more ____ than just a pass - ing

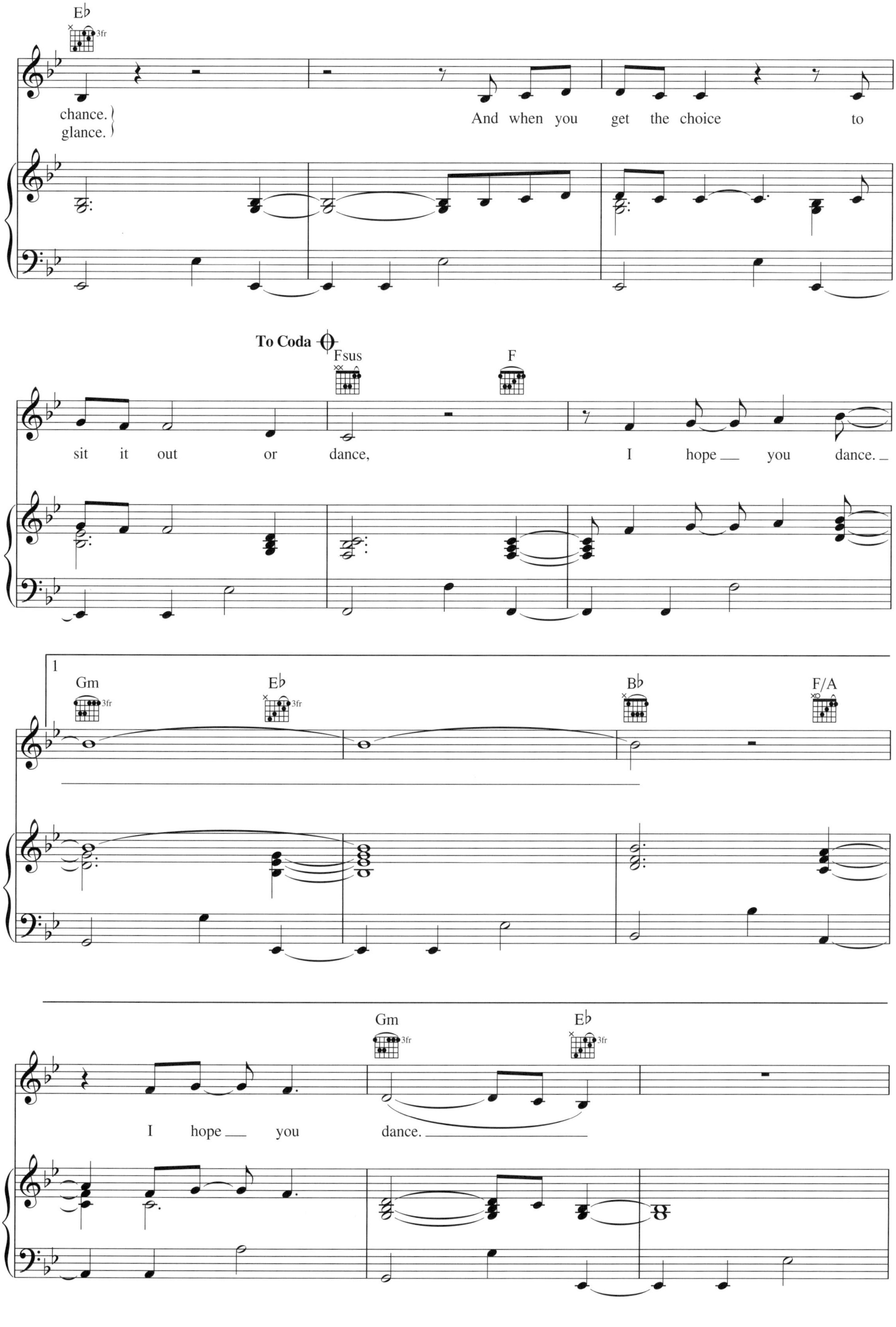

Bb   F/A   Gm   Eb

youth and won - der where ___ those years ___ have ___ gone? ___

___

I hope ___ you dance. ___

Fsus   F   D.S. al Coda
                                                  (Verse 1)   CODA   Fsus

___

I hope ___ you still ___   dance...

Gm   Eb   Bb   F/A

N.C.

Dance, _____

I TRY

Lyrics by MACY GRAY
Music by MACY GRAY, JEREMY RUZUMNA,
JINSOO LIM and DAVID WILDER

Lyrics:

I play it off but I'm dream - ing of you. And I'll keep my cool but I'm fiend-

-in'. I try to say good - bye and I choke. I try to walk a -

way and I stum - ble. Though I try to hide it, it's clear ___ my world

crum - bles when you are not ___ near. Good - bye and I choke. I try to walk a -

Chords: G F#m7 Em7 A D Asus Em7 G A D

Asus **Em7**

way and I stum - ble. Though I try to hide it, it's clear __ my world

G **A** **To Coda** ⊕ **D** **A**

crum-bles when you are not __ near. I may ap - pear to be free but __ I'm just __ a

Em **N.C.** **D**

pris-on - er of your love. And I may seem al - right and smile _____ when you

A **Em7**

leave but __ my smiles are just __ a front, __ just a

front ___ And I play it off but I'm dream - ing of you.

And I'll keep my cool but I'm fiend - in'. I try to say good-

D.S. al Coda

CODA

Here __ is my __ con - fes - sion. May I ___ be your __ pos - ses -

- sion? Boy, __ I need __ your touch, __ your love, __ kiss - es ___ and such. With all _ my might _ I try ___ but this _ I can't _ de - ny, ___ de - ny. _

I play it off but I'm dream - ing of you.

And I'll keep my cool but I'm fiend - in'. ___ I try to say good -

bye and I choke. Try to walk a - way and I stum - ble. Though I try to hide it, it's clear, _ my world crum-bles when you are not _ near. Good-

bye and I choke. Try to walk a-way and I stum-ble. Though I try to

Repeat and Fade

hide it, it's clear, _ my world crum-bles when you are not _ near.

Optional Ending

IF I AIN'T GOT YOU

Words and Music by
ALICIA KEYS

Moderately slow, in one

Some ____ peo - ple live for the
Some ____ peo - ple search for a

for - tune. _____
foun - tain, _____ Some ____ peo - ple
the prom - is - es

live just for the fame. _____
for - ev - er ____ young. _____ You know,

Lyrics:

Gmaj7

Some ___ peo - ple live for the pow - er,
some ___ peo - ple need three doz - en ros -

G#dim7

Am7

___ yeah. ___
es, ___

Some peo - ple live just to play the
and that's the on - ly way to prove you

D7

game. ___
love ___ them.

Gmaj7

Some ___ peo - ple
Hand ___ me the

Am7

think that the vis - i - ble things de -
world on a sil - ver plat - ter, and

Bm7   Am7

Gmaj7
Am7
Bm7
fine what's with - in.
what good would it be
Cmaj7
Bm7
Am7
Gmaj7
Am7
And I've been there be - fore, but
with no one to share, with
Bm7
Am7
Gmaj7
that life's a bore, so full of the
no one who tru - ly cares
Am7
Bm7
su - per - fi - cial.
for me?
Some peo - ple

noth - in' _____ if I ain't got you, _____

1 Gmaj7 **To Coda** ⊕

2 Gmaj7

yeah. _____ you, _____ you, _____ you. _____ Some peo - ple

D.S. al Coda

D/A   G/B

CODA ⊕ Gmaj7

Cmaj7

you, _____ yeah. _____

Bm7

If I ain't got you with me,

ba - by. ___ Said, noth-in' in this

whole wide world don't mean a thing ___ if I ain't got you with me,

ba - by. ___

Freely

I'M WITH YOU

Words and Music by AVRIL LAVIGNE, LAUREN CHRISTY,
SCOTT SPOCK and GRAHAM EDWARDS

Moderately

I'm stand-ing on the bridge. I'm
look-ing for a place. I'm

wait-ing in the dark. I thought that you'd be here ___ by now. There's
search-ing for a face. Is an - y - bod - y here ___ I know? 'Cause

F♯5
D5
5fr
F♯5
noth - ing but the rain. No foot-steps on the ground. I'm lis - ten - ing but there's no
noth - ing's go - ing right and ev - 'ry-thing's a mess. And no one likes to be a -
D5
5fr
E5
Bm
sound.
lone.
Is - n't an - y - one try'n' to find me?
E5
D5
5fr
A5
5fr
B5
D5
5fr
Won't some-bod - y come take me home? It's a damn cold night try'n' to fig-ure
A5
5fr
B5
D5
5fr
A5
5fr
B5
out this life. Won't you take me by the hand, take me

D5 **F#5** **E5** **D(add9)** **F#5**

some-where new. I don't know who you are but I, I'm with you.

D5 **F#5** **D5** **F#5**

I'm with you, ___ umm. _____ I'm you, ___ yeah. __

D5 **E5** **Bm**

_ __ Oh, why is ev-'ry-thing so con-fus-ing?

E5 **Bm** **E5**

May-be I'm just out of my mind, ____ yeah, yeah, ___ yeah, ___

Lyrics beneath the staves:

you. _____ I'm with you. _____

Take me by the hand, take me some-where new. I don't know who you are but

1. I, _____ I'm with

2. I, _____ I'm with you,

oh. I'm with you. _____

I'm with _____ you. _____

I'M LIKE A BIRD

Words and Music by
NELLY FURTADO

Moderately slow

You're

beau-ti-ful, ___ that's for sure.
faith in me ___ brings me to tears

You'll

nev-er, ev-er ___ fade. ___
e-ven af-ter all these ___ years. ___

You're
And it

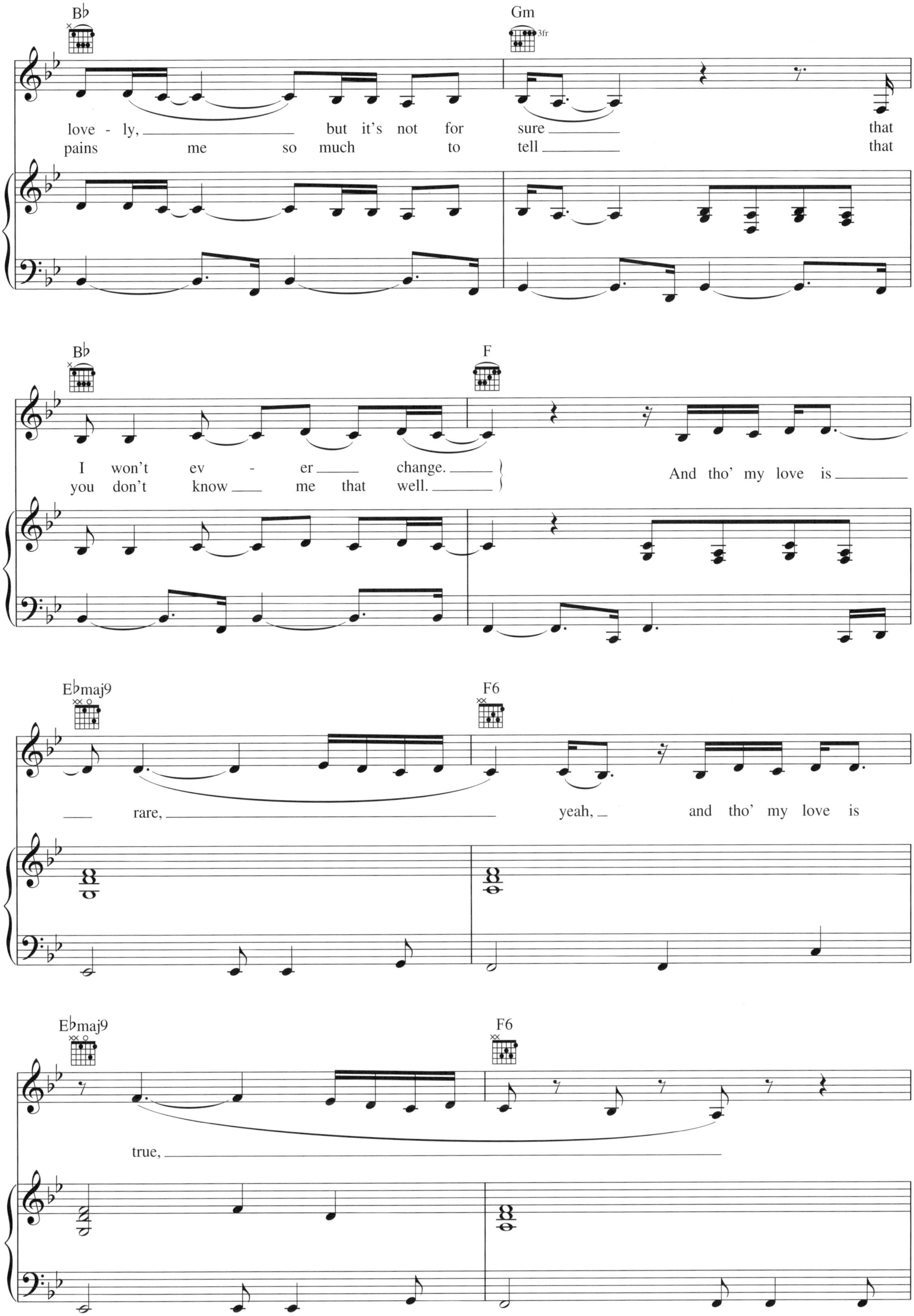

Bb

F6

I'm like __ a bird, ___ I'll on-ly fly a-way. __ I ___ don't know _ where my

Cm

Eb

soul is, I ___ don't know _where my home is. (And, ba-by, all I need for you to

Bb

F6

I'm like __ a bird, ___ I'll on-ly fly a-way. __ I ___ don't know _where my
know is:)

Cm

1

Eb

soul is, I ___ don't know _ where my home is.
(All I need for you to know __ is:)
Your

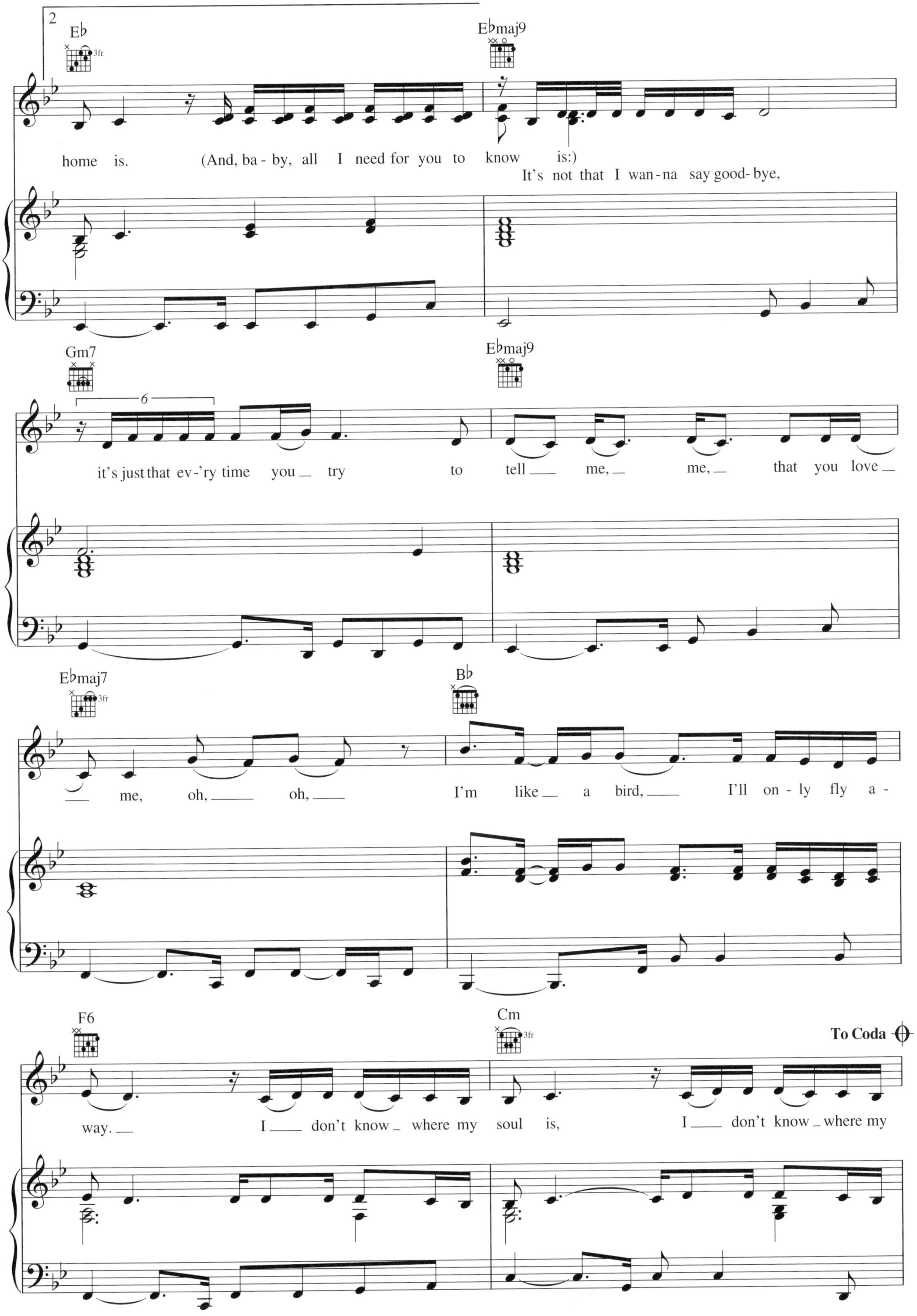

D.S. al Coda
(Verse 2)

CODA

home is.   Your
(All I need for you to know _ is:)

home is.   (And, ba - by, all I need for you to

know   is:)
It's not that I wan - na say good - bye,

it's just that ev-'ry time you _ try   to

tell __ me,   me, __   that you love __ me,   oh, ____   oh, ___

each and ev - 'ry sin - gle day, __   I know I'm gon - na have _ to e - ven-tu - al - ly give __ you __ a - way, __ yeah, yeah, yeah, __ yeah. __

And tho' my love __ is _____ rare, ___ rare, ___ yeah, __

__ yeah, __ and tho' my love __ is true, _____ yeah, __

hey, I'm just ____ scared, _____ yeah, __ yeah, __

that we may fall through woo - woo - woo - woo - woo - woo - woo woo,

yeah, _____ yeah, yeah, _____ yeah. _____

I'm like _ a bird, _____ I _____ don't know _ where my

Cm ... **E♭**

soul is, I ___ don't know ___ where my home is. (And, ba - by, all I need for you to

B♭ ... **F6**

I'm like ___ a bird, ___ I'll on - ly fly a - way. ___ I ___ don't know ___ where my
know is:)

Cm ... **E♭**

Repeat ad lib. and Fade

soul is, I ___ don't know ___ where my home is. (And, ba - by, all I need for you to

I'M YOURS

Words and Music by
JASON MRAZ

Moderately slow, with a Reggae feel

you done done me in; you bet I felt it. I tried to be chill, but you're so hot that I melt ed. I

*Recorded a half step lower.

more.___ It can - not wait. I'm yours.___

Well, o - pen up your mind and see___ like me.___ O - pen up your plans and, damn,___ you're free.

Look in-to your heart _ and you'll _ find love, love, _____ love, love.

Lis-ten to the mu-sic of the mo-ment; peo-ple dance _ and ___ sing. We're just one big fam-i-ly, _

___ and it's our god-for-sak-en right to be loved, _ loved, ___ loved, loved,

loved. _____ So ___ I ___ won't hes-i-tate no more, _ no _____

Am / F

more. _ It can - not wait. I'm sure. _____ There's no

C / G

need ___ to com - pli - cate. Our ___ time ___ is _____

Am / F

short. _ This is our fate. I'm yours. _____ *Scat sing…*

C / G/B / Am / G

Skooch on o - ver clos - er,

F

dear,   and I will nib - ble your ear. _____   *Scat sing...*

D/F#

C   **G/B**   **Am**   **G**

F   **D/F#**

I've been spend - ing

C   **G**

way   too long _ check-ing my tongue in the mir - ror   and bend-ing o - ver back-wards just to try to see it clear - er.   But

Am
my breath fogged _ up the glass, _ and so I drew a new face _ and I laughed. _____ I

C
guess what I'll be say-ing is there ain't no bet-ter rea-son to

G
rid your-self of van-i-ties and just go with the sea-sons. It's

Am
what we aim to do.

F
Our _ name is _ our vir - tue. But

C
I _ won't hes - i - tate no more, _ no _____

C

please don't, please don't, please don't... There's no need to com - pli - cate 'cause our time
need to com - pli - cate. Our time is

G

Am

___ is short. ___ This is, this is, this is our fate. I'm yours. _____ Scat sing...
short. This is our fate. I'm yours.) _____

F   D/F#

C   G

Am   F

Repeat and fade

JESUS WALKS

Words and Music by KANYE WEST,
CURTIS LUNDY, CHE SMITH
and MIRI BEN ARI

Moderate Rap

(Bom, bom, bom, bom bom bom, bom, bom, bom, bom bom...) *(Bass vocal continues)*

(Ooh, ___ ooh.) ___

Spoken: Yo... We at war. We at war with

terrorism, (Ooh, ___ racism, ___ and most of all, ooh.) ___ we at war with ourselves. *(Oohs continue)*

(Je - sus walks,) (Je - sus walks with me, with

Rap 1: *(See additional lyrics)*

* Recorded a half step lower.

me, with me, with me, with me, with me.)

To Coda ⊕

(Je - sus walks,   Je - sus walks with me, with

Chorus: *(See additional lyrics)*

me, with me, with me, with me, with me.) (Je - sus walks,   Je - sus walks,   Je -

sus walks with me, with   me, with me, with me, with me.)   (Je - sus walks,

Je - sus walks.)

(Je - sus walks with me, with me, with me, with me, with me, with me, with me.)

(Je-sus walks _ with them.)

Rap 2: *(See additional lyrics)*

D.S. al Coda

(Je - sus walks _ with them.) _

CODA

- sus walks with me, with me, with me, with me, with me, with me, with...)

Additional Lyrics

Rap 1: God, show me the way, because the Devil's trying to
break me down.

Yeah, oh,
You know what the Midwest is? Young and Restless,
Where restless... might snatch your necklace,
And next these... might jack your Lexus!
Somebody tell these... who Kanye West is.
I walk through the valley of the shadow where death is.
Top floor, the view alone will leave you breathless.
(Uhhh!) Try to catch it! (Uhhh!) It's kinda hard,
Getting choked by detectives, Yeah, yeah, now
  check their method.
They be asking us questions, harass and arrest us,
Saying, "We eat pieces of... like you for breakfast!"
Huh? Y'all eat pieces of...? What's the basis?
We ain't going nowhere, but got suits and cases.
A trunk full of coke, rental car from Avis.
My momma used to say only Jesus could save us.
Well Momma, I know I act a fool,
But I'll be gone till November; I got packs to move.
I hope...

Chorus: God, show me the way, because the Devil's trying to
break me down.
The only thing that I pray is that my feet don't
  fail me now.
And I don't think there's nothing I can do now to right
  my wrongs.
I want to talk to God, but I'm afraid, 'cause we ain't
  spoke in so long.

(Repeat Chorus)

So long...
So long...

Rap 2: To the hustler, killers, murderers, drug dealers,
Even the strippers: (Jesus walks with them.)
To the victims of Welfare, for we living in hell here,
Hell, yeah: (Jesus walks with them.)

Now hear ye, hear ye, want to see Thee more clearly.
I know he hear me when my feet get weary.
'Cause we're the almost nearly extinct.
We rappers is role models; we rap, we don't think.
I ain't here to argue about His facial features,
Or here to convert atheists into believers.
I'm just trying to say the way school need teachers,
The way Kathie Lee needed Regis, that's the way
  I need Jesus.
So here go my single; dog, radio needs this!
They say you can rap about anything except for Jesus.
That means guns, sex, lies, videotapes,
But if I talk about God, my record won't get
  played? Huh?
Well let this take away from my spins,
Which'll probably take away from my ends,
Then I hope it take away from my sins,
And bring the day that I'm dreamin' 'bout.
Next time I'm in the club, everybody screamin' out:

Chorus: God, show me the way, because the Devil's trying to
break me down.
The only thing that I pray is that my feet don't
  fail me now.

JESUS TAKE THE WHEEL

Words and Music by BRETT JAMES,
HILLARY LINDSAY and GORDIE SAMPSON

Moderately slow

She was driv - ing last Fri - day on her way to Cin - cin - nat - i on a
lot on her mind, and she did - n't pay at - ten - tion. She was

snow-white Christ-mas Eve, ___ go - ing home ___ to see her mom - ma and her dad - dy with the
go - ing way too fast; ___ and be - fore ___ she knew it, she was spin - ning on a

ba - by in the back seat. ___ Fif - teen miles to go, ___ and she was run - ning ___ low ___ on
thin black sheet of glass. ___ She saw both their lives ___ flash be - fore her ___ eyes; ___

I'm a - let - ting go; _____ so give me one _ more chance, _

save me from _ this road _____ I'm on. _____

Je - sus, take _ the wheel." _

It was still _

get-ting cold-er when she made it to the shoul-der and the car came to a stop; and she cried

when she saw that ba-by in the back seat, sleep-ing like __ a rock. And for the first

time __ in a long _____ time, __ she bowed her head _ to pray. __ She said, "I'm

sor-ry for _ the way __ I've been liv-ing my life; I know I've got _ to change. __ So from now on, ___ to - night, _____

D.S. al Coda

Je - sus, take ___ the wheel; ___

CODA

Oh, ___ Je - sus take ___ the wheel." ___

"Oh, ___ I'm a - let - ting go; ___ so give me one ___ more ___ chance, save me from ___ this road ___ I'm on, ___

from this road I'm ___ on. ___

Je - sus, take ___ the wheel. ___ Oh, ___ take it,

take it from me." ___ *Vocal continues ad lib.*

KEEP ME IN YOUR HEART

Words and Music by WARREN ZEVON
and JORGE CALDERON

Moderately slow

With pedal

Shad-ows __ are fall-ing and I'm run-ning out __ of breath; __

keep me in __ your heart __ for a-while.

If I leave you, it does-n't mean __ I love you an-y less; __

keep me in _____ your heart for a - while. _____ When you

℅ **G**   **Gmaj7**   **C/G**   **G**

get up in _____ the morn - ing and you see that cra - zy sun, _____
En - gine driv - er's head - ed north to Pleas - ant Stream; _

C/G   **G**

keep me in _____ your heart for a - while. _____ There's a
keep me in _____ your heart for a - while. _____ These

G   **Gmaj7**   **C/G**   **G**

train leav - ing night - ly called _ "When all _____ is said and done;" _
wheels _____ keep turn - ing, but _____ they're run - ning out of steam; _

keep me in ___ your heart for a - while. ___
keep me in ___ your heart for a - while. ___

Sha la la la ___ la la li ___ li li ___ li lo;

keep me in ___ your heart ___ for a - while.

Sha la la la ___ la li li li ___ li lo;

keep me in ___ your heart for a - while. ___

Instrumental solo

To Coda ⊕

Solo ends   Some - times when your do - ing sim - ple things _

a - round ____ the house, ____ may - be ____ you'll think of me ____ and smile. ____

You know I'm tied to you ____ like the

but - tons on your blouse; ____ keep me in ____ your heart for a - while. ____

Hold me in ____ your thoughts, ____

take me to ___ your dreams, ___ touch me as ___ I fall ___ in - to view. ___

___ And when the win - ter comes, ___

keep the fi - res lit, ___ and I will be right ___ next to you.

D.S. al Coda

CODA

Solo ends Keep me in ___ your heart for a - while. ___

rit.

LIKE A STAR

Words and Music by
CORINNE BAILEY RAE

Just like a star a-cross my sky, ___ just like an an-gel off ___ the page, ___ you have ap-
look I can't ___ de - scribe. ___ You make me feel I'm ___ a - live. ___ When ev - 'ry-thing

peared to ___ my life; ___ feel like I'll nev - er be ___ the same. ___ Just like a
else is ___ *au fait,* ___ with - out a doubt you're on ___ my side. ___ Heav - en has

song in ___ my heart, ___ just like oil on ___ my ___ hands... ___ Hon -
been a - way too long! ___ Can't find the words to write ___ this ___ song. ___ Oh, ___

Lyrics (voice line):

da ___ da n da, ___ na na na. Now I have come ___

to un - der - stand ___ the way it is; ___ it's not ___ a se -
I know ___ that you're ___ the on - ly one. ___ I've been ___ con - fused ___

- cret an - y - more, ___ 'cause we've been ___ through that ___ be - fore. ___ From ___ to - night, ___
___ and in ___ the dark; ___ now I un -

- der - stand. ___ Hey, ___ yeah. ___ Ooh. ___

Ooh. ____ I won-der ___ why ___ it

is, ___ I don't ar - gue ___ like ___ this with an - y - one ___

___ but ___ you. ___ I won-der why ___ it is, ___

___ I won't let ___ my ___ guard ___ down for an - y - one ___ but _____ you, ___ ooh. We do it all ___ the time, ___ blow-ing out ___ my mind. _____ Just like a star a-cross ___ my sky, ___ just like an an-gel off ___ the page, ___ you have ap-peared to ___ my life; ___ feel like I'll nev-er be ___ the same. ___ Just like a song in ___ my heart, ___ just like oil on ___ my ___ hands... ___

LIVE LIKE YOU WERE DYING

Words and Music by CRAIG WISEMAN
and TIM J. NICHOLS

He said, "I was in ___

G

__ my ear - ly for - ties with a lot of life __ be - fore __ me when a

C

Em   **D**   **Csus2**

mo - ment came that stopped __ me on a dime. __   I spent

G   **C**

most of the next __ days   look - in' at the x - rays

Em   **D**   **D(add4)**   **Cmaj7**

and talk - in' 'bout the op - tions   and talk - in' 'bout __ sweet __ time." __

Em

I asked him, when it sank in, ___ if this might real-ly be the real end, how's it

G+/D#

G/D

hit you when you get that kind ___ of news? ___

Cmaj9

Man, what'd you do?

N.C.

And he said, "I went sky - div - in', I went

G

C

Rock-y Moun-tain climb - in', I went two-point-sev-en sec - onds on a bull ___

Em **D**

_named Fu _ Man - chu. _ And I loved _ deep - er and I spoke _ sweet - er and I gave for-give - ness I'd _ been de - ny - in'." _ And he said, _ "Some - day _ I hope _ you _ get the chance to live _ like you were dy - in'." _

Lyrics:

He said, "I was fi - nal - ly ___ the hus - band

that most the time I was - n't and I be - came a friend ___ a friend ___ would like to have. ___

___ And all the sud - den go - in' fish - in' was - n't

such an im-po-si-tion and I went ___ three times ___ that year ___ I lost ___ my ___

___ dad. Well, I, I fin-'lly read the Good ___ Book ___ and I

took a good long hard look ___ at what I'd do if I ___ could do ___ it all ___ a-gain. ___

And then I went

D.S. al Coda

CODA

to live __ like you were dy - in', _____ like to-mor-

- row __ was a gift and you got __ e - ter - ni - ty __ to think __

__ a - bout __ what you'd do ____ with it, ___ what could you do __

__ with it, ___ what did I do ___ with it, ___ what would I do __

-er and I watched an ea - gle as __ it was fly -

- in'." __ And he said, __ "Some - day __ I hope __

__ you get the chance __ to live __ like you were dy - in', __

__ to live __ like you were dy - in', __

to live ____ like you were dy - in', ____

to live ____ like you were dy - in', ____

to live ____ like you were dy -

LOVE SONG

Words and Music by
SARA BAREILLES

Head un-der wa-ter, and they tell __ me to breathe eas-y for a while. __ The breath-ing gets hard-er; e-ven I __ know __ that. __

Made room for me. It's too soon to see ___ if I'm hap-

py in your ___ hands. ___ I'm un - u - su'l - ly ___ hard ___ to hold on ___

___ to. ___ Blank stares at

blank pag - es. No eas - y way ___ to say ___ this.

To Coda

Gm   F/A   Dm

write you to stay. _____ If all you have is leav- in', I'm gon-na

G7   B♭sus2   C

need a bet- ter rea- son to write ___ you a love ___ song to- day, _

Gm   F/A   B♭sus2   C   Dm   C/E   F

___ to- day - ay. _____

D/F♯   Gm   F/A   B♭sus2   C   Dm

___ I learned the hard ___ way that they all ___

and dry. Con - vinced me

to please you. Made me think that I need this, too.

I'm try - in' to let you hear me as I am.

D.S. al Coda

I'm not gon - na write you a

Coda

all you have is leav - in', I'm gon - na

need a bet-ter rea-son to write ___ you a love ___ song to - day. ___

Prom - ise ___ me that you'll leave the

light on ___ to help me see ___

with day-light my guide, gone. ___ 'Cause I be - lieve ___

there's a way ____ you can love me, be-cause I say ____ I won't write you a love ____ song 'cause you ask ____ for it, 'cause you need ____ one. You see, ____ I'm not gon-na write you a love song ____ 'cause you tell ____ me it's make or break-in' this. ____ Is that why you want-ed a love song, _____ 'cause you ask _____ for it, 'cause you need _____ one? You see, _____ I'm not gon-na write you a love song _____ 'cause you tell _____ me it's make or break-in' this. _____ If you're on _____ your way, _____ I'm not gon-na write you to stay. _____ If your heart is no-where in it, I don't want it for a min-ute. Babe, I

NOT READY TO MAKE NICE

Words and Music by DAN WILSON,
EMILY ROBISON, MARTIE MAGUIRE
and NATALIE MAINES

For - give, ___ sounds good. For - get, ___ I'm not sure I could. ___ They say ___

* Recorded a half step lower.

Em

D

time heals ev - 'ry - thing, but I'm still

C

wait - ing. I'm through ___

Em

D

___ with ___ doubt. ___ There's

G

C

noth - ing left ___ for me ___ to fig - ure out. I've paid ___

late to make _ it right. _ I prob-'ly would-n't if __ I could, _ 'cause I'm mad as hell, _ can't bring _ my-self _ to do what it is __ you think _ I should. __ I know _____ you said, __ "Can't you just _ get o-

C
Em
- ver it?" It turned my whole world
D
C
a - round and I kind of like it.
Em7
I made my bed and I sleep like a ba - by, with no
D
G
re - grets. And I don't mind say - in' it's a sad, sad sto - ry when a moth-er will teach her daugh-

Lyrics:
-ter that she ought to hate a per-fect stran - ger. And how ___ in the world can the words that I said

send some-bod - y so o - ver the edge ___ that they'd write me a let - ter, say - in' that I bet - ter

shut up and sing or my life will be o - ver? ___

Lyrics (vocal line):

I'm not ready to make_ nice, __ I'm not read-y to back_ down. __ I'm still mad as hell_ and I don't_ have time_ to go round and round_ and round. _ It's too late to make_ it right. _ I prob-'ly would-n't if __ I could, _ 'cause I'm mad as hell,_ can't bring_ my-self_ to do what it is_ you think_ I should._

I'm not what it is_ you think_ I should,_

what it is_ you think_ I

should.

For - give, _____ sounds

good. For - get, _____ I'm not sure ___ I could. _

They say _____ time heals

ev - 'ry - thing, but I'm still wait - ing.

ORDINARY PEOPLE

Words and Music by JOHN STEPHENS
and WILL ADAMS

Moderately fast

Hoh, _____ hoh. _____

Girl, __ I'm in love with you, __

but this __ ain't the hon-ey-moon. __ We're past the in-fat-u-a-tion

Fadd2 B♭maj7 E♭maj9

phase.　　　　　We're right _ in the thick of love. _　　　At times _ we get sick of love. _

Fmaj13 B♭maj7

It seems _ like we ar-gue ev-'ry day. _　　　I know I've _ mis - be - haved _ and you've made _

E♭maj9 Fmaj9

_ your mis-takes _ and we've both _ still got room _ left to grow. _　　　And though love _

B♭maj7 E♭maj9

_ some-times hurts, _ I still _ put you first. _ And we'll make _ this thing work, _ but I think _

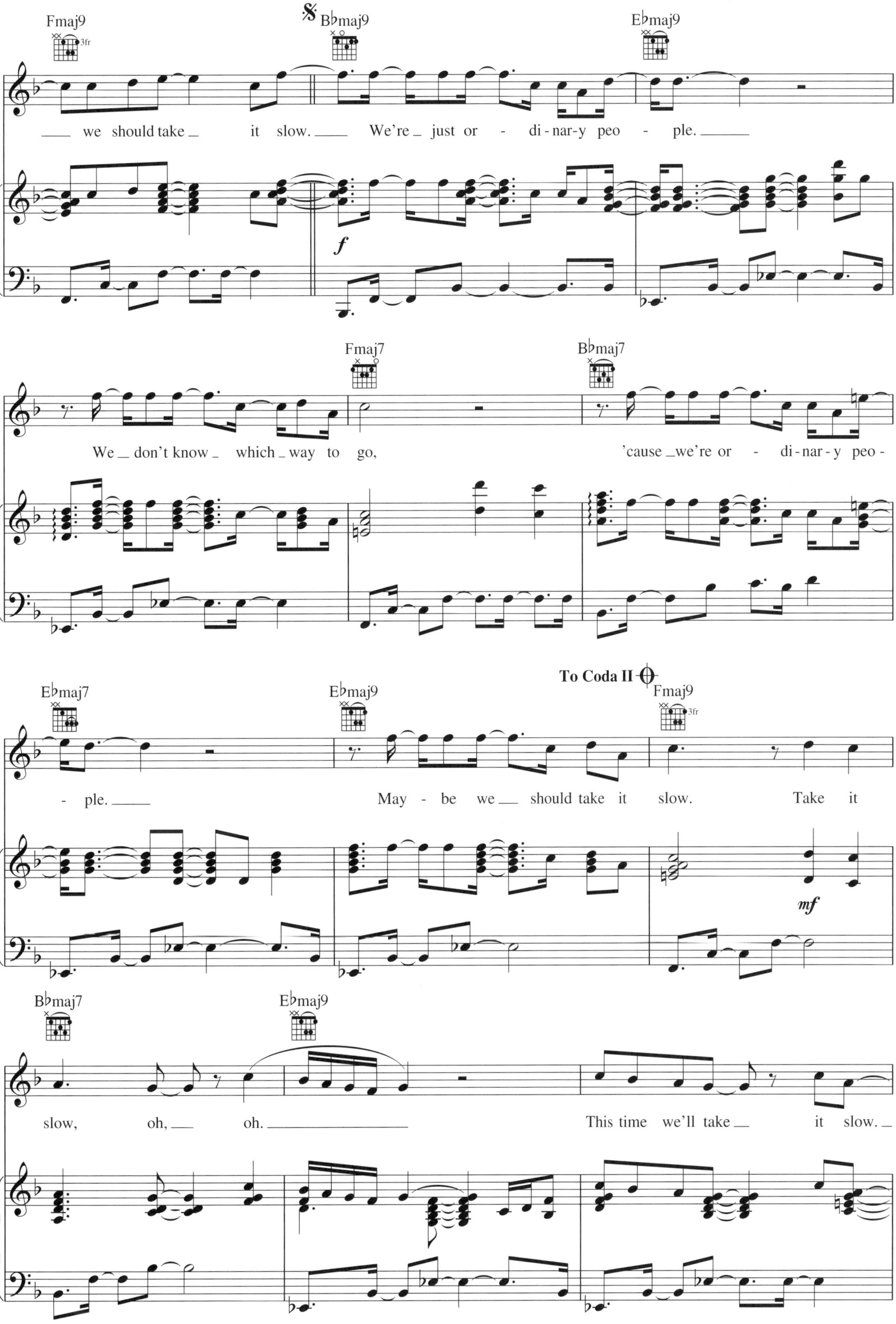

To Coda I

I hang ___ up; you call. ___ We rise ___ and we fall, ___ and we feel ___ like just walk - ing a - way. ___ But as our ___ love ad - vanc - es, we take ___ sec - ond chanc - es. Though it's ___ not a fan - ta - sy, I ___ still want you ___ to stay. ___

D.S. al Coda I

Coda I

This time we'll take ___ it slow. ___ Take it slow. ___ May - be we'll live and learn.

May - be we'll crash and burn. __ May - be you'll stay; may - be you'll leave; may - be you'll re - turn. __

May - be an - oth - er fight; __ may - be we won't sur - vive.

D.S. al Coda II

But may - be we'll grow. We __ nev - er know, ba - by, you _____ and I. __

Coda II

slow. Take it slow, oh, __ oh. _____

This time we'll take __ it slow. __ Take it __ Take it

slow, __ slow. __ This time we'll take __ it

slow. Take it slow, oh, __ oh. __

This time we'll take __ it slow. __

POKER FACE

Words and Music by STEFANI GERMANOTTA
and RedOne

Dance Pop

I wan - na hold 'em like they do in Tex - as plays:
I wan - na roll with him, a hard pair we will be.

Am
F/A
G
fold 'em, let 'em hit me, raise it. Ba - by, stay with me.
A lit - tle gam - bl - in' is fun when you're with me.
Am
F/A
G
Luck and in - tu - i - tion play the cards with spades to start. And
Rus - sian Rou - lette is not the same with - out a gun. And,
Am
F/A
G
af - ter he's been hooked, I'll play the one that's on his heart.
ba - by, when it's love, if it's not rough it is - n't fun.
Am
F/A
G
Am
Oh, whoa, oh, oh, oh, oh, oh. I'll get him hot, show

him what I got. __ Oh, whoa, __ oh, oh, oh, _____ oh,

oh. I'll get him hot, show him what I got. __ Can't read my, __ can't read my, __

__ no, he can't read __ my pok - er face. __ (She's got to love no-bod-y.)

Can't read my, __ can't read my, ___ no, he can't read __ my pok - er face. __

F/A
G
Am
hug you 'cause I'm bluff - in' with my muf - fin. I'm not ly - in', I'm just
F/A
G
Am
stun - nin' with my love glue - gun - nin'. Just like a chick in the ca -
F/A
G
Am
si - no, take your bank be - fore I pay you out. I prom - ise this, prom -
F/A
G
Am
ise this. Check this hand, 'cause I'm mar - vel - ous.
Can't read my, can't read my,

PRETTY WINGS

Words and Music by MUSZE
and HOD DAVID

Slow half-time groove

Time will bring the real ____ end of our trial. ____ One
Your ____ face will be the rea - son I smile, ____ but

day there'll be no rem - nants, no trace, ____ no re - sid - u - al ____ feel -
I will not see what I can - not ____ have for - ev - er. I'll ____

- ings with - in ya. One day you won't re - mem -
____ al - ways love ya; I hope you feel the same. ____

Amaj9 **C#m7** **Amaj9**

a - way   from   me,   to   see   clear - ly   the   way   that

Esus2/G# **Amaj9** **E(add2)**

love   can   be ___ when   you ___ are   not _____ with   me.   I   had   to

Amaj9 **Esus2/G#** **Amaj9**

leave,   I   had   to   live.   I   had   to   leave, ___ I   had   to

(If

F#m11

live.   I   can't   have ___ you,   let   love   set   you   free   to   flap   your

love ___ in - to ___ lie. ___ Ba - by, be - lieve ___ me, ___ I'm

sor - ry I told ___ you lies. ___ I ___ turned ___ day ___

___ in - to ___ night; ___ sleep ___ till I die ___ a thou - sand times. ___

___ I ___ should have showed ___ you bet - ter nights, ___

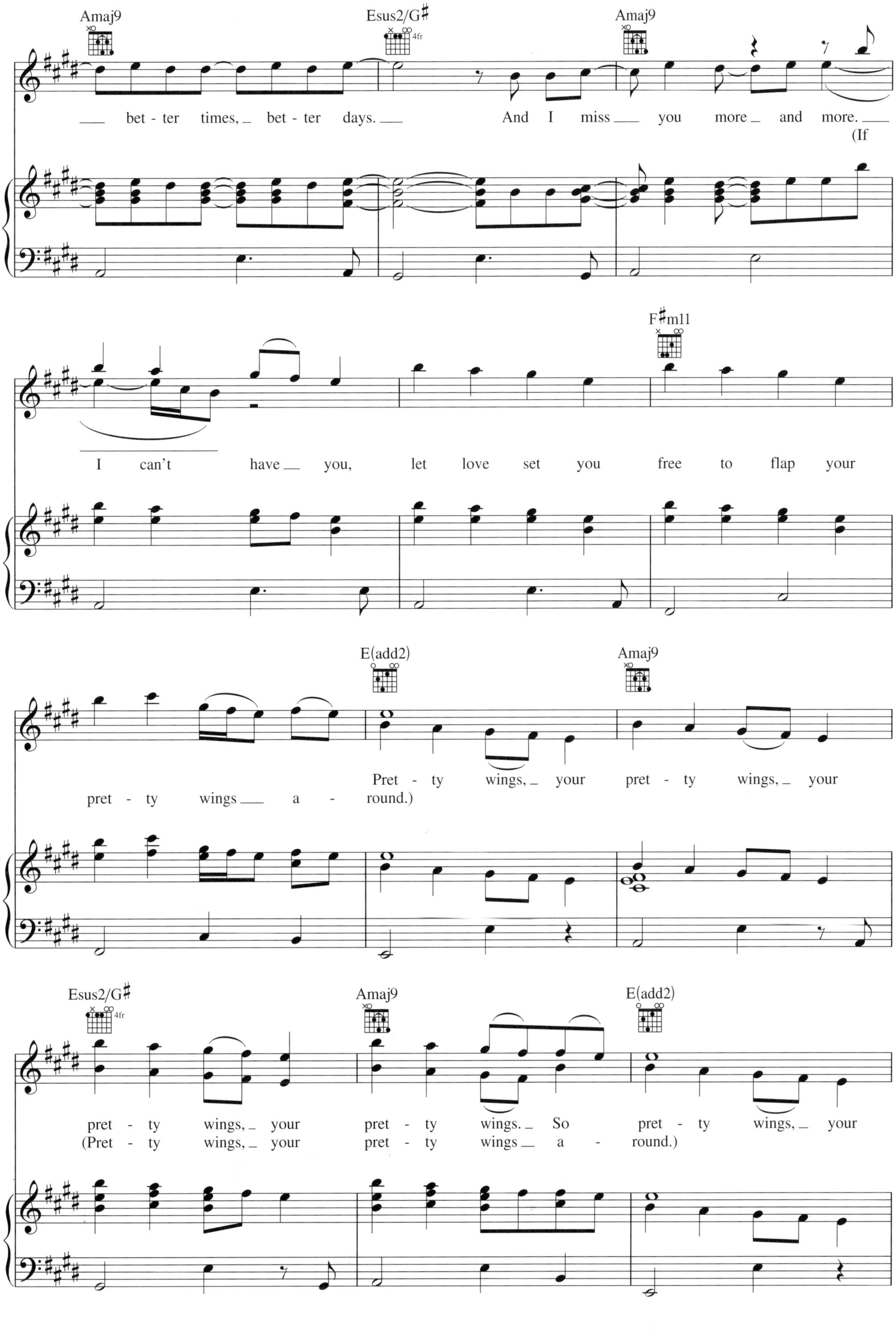

pret - ty wings, _ your pret - ty wings, _ your pret - ty wings. _ Sing
(Pret - ty wings, _ your pret - ty wings _ a -

pret - ty wings, _ oh, pret - ty _ wings, yeah, _ (Pret - ty wings, _ your
round.)

pret - ty wings _ a - round.
a - round.)

Lead vocal ad lib.

PUT YOUR RECORDS ON

Words and Music by JOHN BECK,
STEVEN CHRISANTHOU and CORINNE BAILEY RAE

Moderately

Three ___ lit - tle birds sat on my win - dow
Blue ___ as the sky, sun - burnt and lone - ly,

and they told me I don't need to wor - ry. ___
sip - pin' tea in a bar by the road - side. ___

B9/F#

Sum - mer came like cin - na - mon, so _____ sweet.
Don't you let those oth - er boys fool _____ you,

D/E   E9   A   F#m

Lit - tle girls dou - ble dutch on the con - crete. _____   May - be some-
got - ta love that _____ Af - ro _____ hair - do. _____   May - be some-

F#m(maj7)/E#   F#m7   B7

- times _____ we _____ got it wrong, but it's al - right. _____ The more _____
- times _____ we _____ feel a - fraid, but it's al - right. _____ The more _____

Dmaj7   Dm(maj7)

_____ things seem _____ to change, _____ the more _____ they stay the same. Oo, _____
_____ you stay _____ the same, _____ the more _____ they seem to change.

Lyrics:

'Twas more than I could take, __ pit-y for pit-y's sake. __ Some nights kept me a-wake, __

I thought that I was strong-er. __ When you gon-na re-al-ize __

that you don't e-ven have to try an-y long-er? Do __ what you want to. __

Girl, put your rec-ords on. __ Tell me your fav-'rite song. __

Chords: Bm7, F#m7, Bm7, Dmaj7, Bm7, Dmaj7, E7, A, B9/F#

THE REASON

Words and Music by DANIEL ESTRIN
and DOUGLAS ROBB

Moderately slow

1. I'm not a per-fect per-son,
2. I'm sor-ry that I hurt you,

there's man-y things I wish I did-n't do.
it's some-thing I must live with ev-'ry-day.

E

But I con - tin - ue learn -
And all the pain __ I put you __
3. I'm not a per - fect __ per -

C#m

- ing. __ I nev - er meant __ to do __ those things __ to you. __
__ through, __ I wish that I __ could take __ it all __ a - way. __
- son. __ I nev - er meant __ to do __ those things __ to you. __

A9

__ And so, I have __ to say __ be - fore __ I go, __
__ And be the one __ who catch - es all __ your tears. __
__ And so, I have __ to say __ be - fore __ I go, __

B

__ that I just want you to know __
__ That's why I need you to hear. __
__ that I just want you to know __

I've found a rea - son for me

to change who I used to be.

A rea - son to start o - ver

To Coda ⊕

new,

and the rea - son is

new,

and the rea - son is ___

you,
(you, ___

and the rea - son is ___ you.
is ___ you, ___

And the rea - son is ___ you,
is ___ you, ___

D.S. al Coda

and the rea - son is ___ you.
is ___)

CODA

B

new,

and the rea - son is ____

E

you.

I've found ___ a ___ rea - son to show _____ a

C#m

A(add2)

side ___ of ___ me ___ you did-n't know,

a rea - son ___ for all that ___ I

B

do,

and the rea - son is ____ you.

E

rit.

SINGLE LADIES
(Put a Ring on It)

Words and Music by BEYONCÉ KNOWLES,
THADDIS HARRIS, CHRISTOPHER STEWART
and TERIUS NASH

Moderate groove

All the sin-gle la-dies, all the sin-gle la-dies. All the

sin-gle la-dies, all the sin-gle la-dies. All the sin-gle la-dies, all the sin-gle la-dies. All the

sin-gle la-dies, now put your hands up.

Up in the club, we just broke up. I'm
gloss for my lips, a man on my hips, hold me

do - in' my own lit - tle thing.
tight - er than my De - re - on___ jeans.

You de - cid - ed to dip and now you wan-na trip 'cause an-
Act - in'___ up,___ drink___ in my cup,___

oth - er broth - er no - ticed me.
I can care___ less what you think.

I'm up on him, he up on me. Don't
I need no per-mis - sion. Did I men - tion? Don't

pay him an - y at - ten - tion.___ Just cried my tears for three good years, you
pay him an - y at - ten - tion.___ 'Cause you had your turn and now you gon' learn what it

E5

can't be mad at me.
real-ly feels___ like to miss___ me.

'Cause if you like it then you should have put a ring on it.___ If you like it then you should have put a ring on it. ___ Don't be mad ___ once you see ___ that he want it. ___ If you

like it then you should have put a ring on it. Oh, oh, oh, oh, oh, oh, oh, ___ oh,

oh, oh, oh, oh. Oh, oh, oh, oh, oh, oh, oh, ___ oh, oh, oh, oh, oh. If you

B5 **C+(no3)** **B5** **A5**

like it then you should have put a ring on it. ___ If you like it then you should have put a ring on it. ___ Don't be

Lyrics:

___ is what ___ I pre-fer, ___ what ___ I de-serve. _____ Here's a man ___ that makes ___

___ me ___ then takes ___ me ___ and de-liv - ers me ___ to a des - ti - ny, ___ to in-fin-

- i-ty ___ and be-yond. ___ Pull me in - to your arms, ___ say I'm ___

___ the one ___ you want. ___ If you don't, ___ you'll be a - lone ___ and like a ghost ___

I'll be gone. All the sin-gle la-dies,_ all_ the sin-gle la-dies._ All_ the

sin-gle la-dies,_ all_ the sin-gle la-dies._ All_ the sin-gle la-dies,_ all_ the sin-gle la-dies._ All_ the

sin-gle la-dies,_ now put your hands up. Oh, oh, oh, oh, oh, oh, oh,_ oh,

oh, oh, oh, oh. Oh, oh, oh, oh, oh, oh, oh,_ oh, oh, oh, oh, oh. Oh, oh,
'Cause if you

like it then you should have put a ring on it. ___ If you like it then you should have put a ring on it. ___ Don't be

mad ___ once you see ___ that he want it. ___ If you like it then you should have put a ring on it. Oh, oh, 'Cause if you

like it then you should have put a ring on it. Oh, oh, oh.

REHAB

Words and Music by
AMY WINEHOUSE

Retro Blues

They tried to make me go to re - hab, I ___ said, ___ "No, ___ no, ___ no."

Yes, ___ I been ___ black, but when ___ I come ___ back, you won't

know, ___ know, ___ know. ___ I ain't got the time, ___

F7

and if my dad - dy ____ thinks ____ I'm fine, _____ he's

C7(no3rd)   F7   C7(no3rd)

tried to make me go to re - hab, ___ I ____ won't ____ go, _____ go, _____ go. ___

Em

I'd rath - er be   at home _____
The man said, "Why   you think _____
I won't ev - er   want to ___ drink _____

Am

with Ray,
you're here?"
a - gain,

F

I ain't
I said,
I just,

Fm/Ab

got sev - en - ty days.
"I got no i - de - a,
oo, I just need a friend.

'Cause there's
I'm
I'm not

Em

noth - ing,
gon - na,
gon - na

there's noth - ing you can teach me
I'm gon - na lose my ba - by,
spend ten weeks,

Am

F

that I can't learn from Mis - ter
so I al - ways keep a
have ev - 'ry - one think I'm

Fm/A♭
G7
Hath - a - way. I did - n't
bot - tle near." Said, "I just
on the mend.
get a lot in class, but I
think you're de - press - ed,
It's not just my pride,
F7
To Coda
know it don't come in a
kiss me, ba - by, and go
it's just 'til these tears have
C7(no3rd)
shot glass. They
rest." They tried to make me go to re - hab, I said,

"No, _____ no, _____ no." _____ Yes, _____ I been _____ black, but when _____

D.S. al Coda

_____ I come _____ back, you won't know, _____ know, _____ know. _____

CODA

C7(no3rd)

dried. _____ They tried to make me go to re-

- hab, _____ I _____ said, _____ "No, _____ no, _____ no." _____ Yes, _____

THE RISING

Words and Music by
BRUCE SPRINGSTEEN

Moderately ♩ = 108

*Tune guitar
a half
step down* ⟶

Piano ⟶

Verse:

E(9) / E♭(9)   B(9) / B♭(9)   E(9) / E♭(9)

1. Can't see noth-in' in front___ of me,
3. *See additional lyrics*

can't see noth - in' com - ing_

mf

B(9) / B♭(9)   E(9) / E♭(9)   B(9) / B♭(9)

___ up be - hind.___   I make my way___ through this dark - ness.___   I

E(9) / E♭(9)   B(9) / B♭(9)   E(9) / E♭(9)

can't feel noth-ing but this chain___ that binds___ me.

(1.) Lost track of how far___
2. 3. *See additional lyrics*

I've gone, how far I've gone,___ how___ high___ I've climbed.

On my back's a six - ty pound___ stone,___ on my shoul-der a half mile___

Chorus:

___ of line.___ Come on up___ for the ris - ing.___

Come on up,___ lay your hands___ in mine.___ Come on up___ for the ris -

Bridge:

...*end solo*) There's spir - its a - bove___ and be - hind___ me, fac -

es gone black, eyes burn - in' bright. May their pre - cious blood___ bind___

Coda

Sky of black - ness and sor - row.___ (A dream of life.) Sky of love,___ sky

of tears. (A dream of life.) Sky of glo - ry and sad - ness.___ (A dream of life.)

Sky of mer - cy, sky___ of fear. (A dream of life.) Sky of mem - 'ry and shad-

ows.___ (A dream of life.) Your burn - ing wind___ fills my___ arms to - night. (A dream of life.)

Sky of long - ing and emp - ti - ness.___ (A dream of life.) Sky of full - ness, sky of___ ___ bless - ed life. Come on up___ for the ris - ing.___

Chorus:

Come on up,___ lay your hands___ in mine.___ Come on up___ for the ris - ing.___ Come on up___ for the ris - ing to - night.___ Li___

Verse 2:
Left the house this morning,
Bells ringing filled the air.
Wearin' the cross of my callin'.
On wheels of fire I come rollin' down here.
(To Chorus:)

Verse 3:
I see you, Mary, in the garden,
In the garden of a thousand sighs.
There's holy pictures of our children,
Dancin' in a sky filled with light.
May I feel your arms around me,
May I feel your blood mixed with mine.
A dream of life comes to me,
Like a catfish dancin' on the end of my line.
Sky of blackness and sorrow... etc.
(To Coda)

SAY MY NAME

Words and Music by RODNEY JERKINS,
LASHAWN DANIELS, FRED JERKINS,
BEYONCÉ KNOWLES, KELENDRIA ROWLAND,
LATAVIA ROBERSON and LETOYA LUCKETT

name.

An - y oth - er day   I would call,   you would say,   "Ba - by, how's your day?"   But to-
What is   up with this?   Tell the truth,   who're you with?   How would you like it if   I came

day   it ain't the same.   Ev - 'ry oth - er word   is "Uh huh,   yeah, o - kay."
o - ver with   my   clique?   Don't   try to change it   now,   say   you   got - ta bounce,   when

Could it   be that you   are at the   crib with an-oth-er la - dy?   If you   took it there,   first of
two sec-onds a - go   you said you just got   in   the house.   It's   hard to be - lieve that you   are at

all,   let me say,   I am not the one   to sit a - round   and be played.   So
home   by your- self,   when I   just heard the voice,   heard   the voice of some - one   else.

Cm · A♭ · Fm

prove your-self to me: If I'm the girl that you claim, why don't you say the things that you
Just this ques- tion: Why, do you feel you got-ta lie? Get-ting caught up in your game, when you

Fm7/B♭ · G7♭9/B · Cm

said to me yes- ter- day? }
can - not say my name. } I know you say that I am as-sum-ing things. _

A♭ · Fm

Some-thing's go-ing down, that's the way it seems. _ Should-n't be no rea-son why you're act-ing strange _ if

Fm7/B♭ · Bdim7 · Cm

no-bod-y's hold-ing you back from me. _ 'Cause I know how you u-sua'ly do, _ where you're

Ab

say- ing ev-'ry-thing to me times two. Why can't you just tell the truth?_ If

Fm

Fm7/Bb   **Bdim7**   **Cm**

some- bod- y's there, then tell me who. _____

change? Say my name,_ say my

Say my name, say my

Ab   **Fm**   **Fm7/Bb**   **Bdim7**

name. If } no one is a- round, you say, "Ba- by, I love you." If you ain't run- ning

name. When

Cm   **Ab**   **Fm**   **To Coda**

game, say my name, say my name. You're act- ing kind- a shad- y, ain't call- ing me

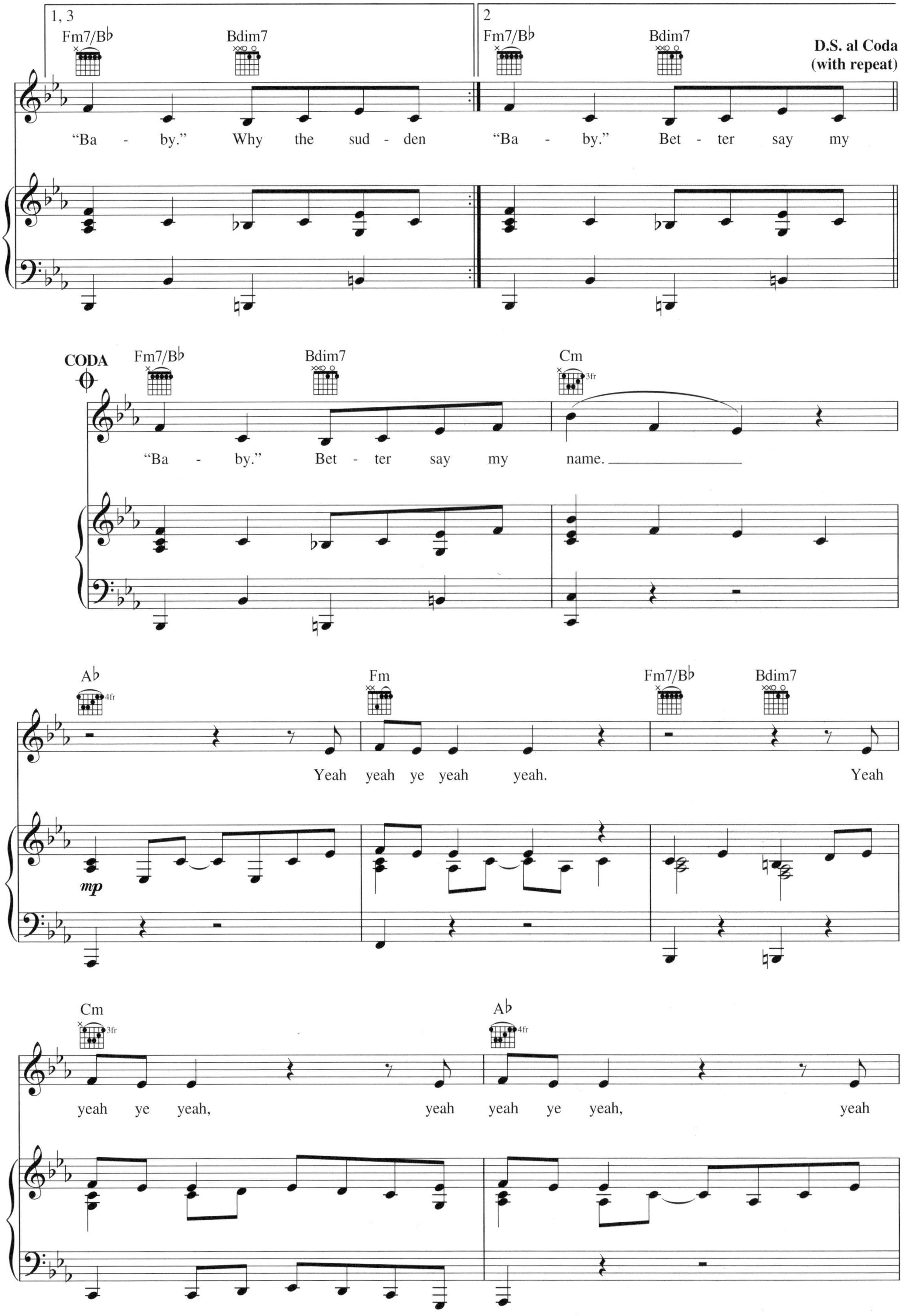

Cm
know you say that I am as-sum-ing things. __ Ab Some-thing's go-ing down, that's the way it seems. __

Fm
Should-n't be no rea-son why you're act-ing strange __ if Fm7/Bb no-bod-y's hold-ing you back from me. __ Bdim7 'Cause

Cm
I know how you u-sua'ly do, __ Ab where you're say-ing ev-'ry-thing to me times two.

Fm
Why can't you just tell the truth? __ If Fm7/Bb some-bod-y's there, then tell me who. __ Bdim7

Ab

change? } Say my name, __ say my name. { (1., 3.) If } no one is a-
name. }   { (2., 4.) When }

Fm   **Fm7/Bb**   **Bdim7**

round,   you   say, "Ba - by,   I   love   you."   If   you ain't run - ning

Cm   **Ab**

game,   say   my   name,   say   my   name.   You're act - ing kind - a

Fm   **Fm7/Bb**   **Bdim7**   **Play 4 times** N.C.

shad - y,   ain't call - ing me "Ba - by." { (1., 3.) Why the sud - den
                                              { (2., 4.) Bet - ter say my   name.

SOMETIMES YOU CAN'T MAKE IT ON YOUR OWN

Words by BONO
Music by U2

Lis - ten to __ me now. __ I

need to let __ you know _____ you don't have to go it a - lone. __

And it's you __ when I look in the mir -

ror, and it's you __ when I don't pick up the phone. __ Some-

- times you can't make __ it on your own. __

We

I know that we don't talk. I'm sick of __ it all.

Can you __ hear __ me when I __

sing? _____ You're the rea - son I sing. _____

You're the rea - son why _____ the op -

- era is in ___ me... Where are we now?

Still got to let ___ you know a house still does-n't make a home. _

Don't leave me here a - lone... And it's you when I look in the mir - ror, and it's you that makes it hard to let go. Some - times you can't make it on your own.

Lyrics:
Some - times you can't make _ it, best you can do is to fake _ it. Some - times you can't make _ it on _ your own. _

VIVA LA VIDA

Words and Music by GUY BERRYMAN, JON BUCKLAND,
WILL CHAMPION and CHRIS MARTIN

Moderately

I used to rule the world. __

__ Seas would rise when I gave the word. __ Now in the morn-ing I

sleep a - lone, __ sweep the streets I used to own. __

Lyrics:

I used to roll the dice, ___ feel the fear in my en-e-mies' eyes. ___

___ Lis-ten as the crowd ___ would sing, ___
sound ___ of drums. ___

"Now the
Peo-ple

Ab   Fm   Db5   Eb7sus

old king is dead, __ long live the king." One min-ute I held the key, __
could-n't be-lieve __ what I'd be-come. Rev-o-lu-tion-ar - ies wait __

Ab   Fm

__ next the walls were closed on me. And I dis-cov-ered that my
__ for my head on a sil-ver plate.__ Just a pup-pet on a

Db5   Eb7sus   Ab   Fm

cas - tles stand ___ up - on pil-lars of salt __ and pil-lars
lone - ly string.__ Ah, __ who would ev-er wan-na be king?__

Db5   Eb7sus

of sand. __ I hear
I hear } Je-ru-sa-lem bells __ a - ring - ing,
(D.S.) Hear }

Ro - man Cath - o - lic choirs __ are sing - ing. Be my mir - ror, my sword __

__ and shield, __ my mis - sion - ar - ies in a for - eign field. __

For some rea - son I can't __ ex - plain. __ {(2.,3.) I know Saint Pe - ter won't

(1.) Once you've gone there was

nev - er, nev - er an hon - est word. __ And that was

call my name, nev - er an hon - est word. __ But that was

when I ruled the world. _____
when I ruled the world. _

It was a wick-ed and wild _____ wind _

_____ blew down the doors to let me in. _____ Shat-tered win-dows and the

D.S. al Coda

oh.

CODA

hon - est word.

But that was when I ruled the world.

Optional Ending

Repeat and Fade

Ooh.

STUCK IN A MOMENT YOU CAN'T GET OUT OF

Lyrics by BONO and THE EDGE
Music by U2

Moderately slow

I'm not a-fraid ___ of an-y-thing in ___ this world. ___ There's noth-ing you can throw at me ___ that I

A(add2)
E
E/G♯
have-n't al-read-y heard.
I'm just try-in' to find a de-
A
E/G♯
B
C♯m
4fr
-cent mel-o-dy, a song that I can sing in my
A
E
E/G♯
A
E/G♯
own com-pa-ny.
You've got to get your-self to-geth-er. You got
B
C♯m
4fr
A
E
stuck in a mo-ment and now you can't get out of it.

Don't say that lat-er will be bet-ter. Now you're

stuck in a mo-ment and you can't get out ___ of it.

I will not ___ for-sake ___ the col-

-ors that you bring, ___ the nights ___ you filled with fire-works they, they

A E E/G♯
left you with noth - ing.
I am still en - chant - ed by the
A E/G♯ B C♯m7
light you brought to me.
Lis - ten through your ears.
Through
A E E/D♯ C♯m A
your eyes I could see.
You are such a fool
F♯7 A C♯m
to wor - ry like you do.
Oh.
I know it's tough,

and you can nev - er get e - nough of what you don't real - ly need

now. My, oh my. ____ You've got to

get your - self to - geth - er. You've got stuck in a mo - ment and you

can't get out ____ of it. Oh Lord,

look at you now; ___ you've got your-self stuck in a mo - ment and you

can't get out ___ of it. I was un - con - scious, half ___ a - sleep. The

wa - ter is warm ___ 'til you dis-cov - er how deep. _____

I was-n't jump - ing; for me it was a fall. It's a

long way down to noth - ing at all. _____ Oh hey,

you've got to get your - self to - geth - er. You've got

stuck in a mo - ment and you can't get out ___ of it.

Don't say that lat - er will be bet - ter. Now you're

stuck in a mo - ment and you can't get out __ of it. (And if the night __ __ runs o - ver, and if the day __ won't last, __ and if your way __ should fal - ter a - long the ston - it's just a mo - ment; this time will pass. __ - y pass), __

A THOUSAND MILES

Words and Music by
VANESSA CARLTON

Moderately

Mak-ing my way __ down - town, __ walk - ing fast. __ Fac - es pass __ and I'm home - bound.

*Recorded a half step higher.

Star-ing blank-ly a-head,__ just mak-ing my way,__ mak-ing a way____ through__ the

crowd. _____

And I need you   and I'll miss you,
'Cause I need you   and I'll miss you,
And I still need you   and I still miss you,

To Coda ⊕

and now I won - der,   if

(1.) It's

al-ways times_ like these_ when I think_ of you___ and I won - der if___ you ev - er

think of ___ me. ___

'Cause

ev - 'ry - thing's_ so wrong_ and I don't_ be - long___ liv - ing in ___ your pre - cious

Gm7 F/A F7sus

D.S. al Coda

CODA Eb(add9) F

I, _____ I _____ don't. _____

won - der,

if I could _ fall _ in - to the _ sky, _ do

you think _ time _____ would pass us _____ by? 'Cause

you know _ I'd _____ walk _ a thou - sand _ miles _ if I could

Lyrics: just see _____ you, if I could just hold _____ you to - night. _____

UMBRELLA

Words and Music by SHAWN CARTER,
THADDIS L. HARRELL, CHRISTOPHER STEWART
and TERIUS NASH

Moderate Hip-Hop

Rap: (See rap lyrics)

Eh,   eh,   eh.

eh,   eh,   eh,   eh.

* Recorded a half step lower.

F♯m7
Bm9
Eh, eh, eh, eh, eh, eh, eh. You
Gmaj7
A
had my heart and we'll nev - er be worlds a - part. May be in
F♯m7
Bm9
mag - a - zines, but you'll still be my star. Ba - by, 'cause
Gmaj7
A
in the dark you can see shin - y cars and that's when you

need me there. __ With you I'll al-ways share be-cause __

__ when the sun shines, we'll shine to-geth-er. Told you I'll be here for-ev-

er. Said I'll al-ways be your friend. __ Took an oath, I'm-a stick it out 'til the end. __

__ Now that it's rain-in' more than ev-er, know that we'll still have each oth-er. You can stand un-der my um-br-el - la. You can stand un-der my um-br-el-

la, el - la, el - la, eh, eh, eh. Un-der my um-br-el - la, el - la, el - la, eh,

eh, eh. Un-der my um-br-el - la, el - la, el - la, eh, eh, eh. Un-der my um-brel-

To Coda

la, el - la, el - la, eh, eh, eh, eh, eh, eh. These fan - cy things __ will nev-er come in be - tween. __ You're part of my en - ti - ty, __ here for in -

fin - i - ty. __ When the war has took its part, __ when the world has

dealt its cards, __ if the hand is hard, __ to - geth - er we'll

mend your heart. __ Be - cause, __

CODA

eh, eh, eh, eh, eh.

D.S. al Coda

You can run __ in - to __ my arms. __ It's o - kay, __ don't be __ a - larmed. __ Come

in - to me, there's no dis-tance in _____ be - tween _ our love. __ Gon - na let the rain __

fall. I'll be all you need and more. _____ Be - cause,

when the sun shines, we'll shine to-geth - er. Told you I'll be here for-ev - er. Said I'll al-ways be your friend. __

la, el - la, el - la, eh, eh, eh. Un - der my um - br - el - la, el - la, el - la, eh,

eh, eh, eh, eh, eh. It's rain - in', rain - in'. Ooh, ba - by, it's rain - in', rain - in'. Ba - by, come

in - to me, ____ come in - to me. ____ **Repeat and Fade** It's rain - in'. ____

Optional Ending

Rap Lyrics

No clouds in my storms. Let it rain. I hydroplane into fame.
Comin' down with the Dow Jones. When the clouds come, we gone.
We Rockafella, she fly higher than weather and she rocks it better.
You know me. An anticipation for precipitation. Stack chips for the rainy day.
Jay, rain man is back wit' little Miss Sunshine. Rihanna, where you at?

USE SOMEBODY

Words and Music by CALEB FOLLOWILL, NATHAN FOLLOWILL,
JARED FOLLOWILL and MATTHEW FOLLOWILL

Oh, _____ oh. _____

I've been roam-in' a-round, ___ I was look-in' down ____ at all ___ I see. ___

Paint-ed fac - es fill ___ the plac -

- es I ____ can't reach. ___ You know ___ that I could

use some - bod - y. _____

You know ___ that I could use some - bod - y. _____

Some - one ___ like you _____ and all ___ you know ___
_____ while you live it ___ up,

___ and how ___ you speak. ___ Count - less lov -
___ I'm off ___ to sleep. ___ Wag - in' wars ___

C

ers un - der cov - er of ___ the street. ___
___ to shake ___ the po - et and ___ the beat. ___

C/E

F6

Am7

You know ___ that I could use some - bod - y. ___
I hope ___ it's gon - na make you no - tice, ___

Csus2

F6

You know ___ that I could use some - bod - y, ___
I hope ___ it's gon - na make you no - tice ___

Am7

Csus2

F6

___
___

some - one ___ like you.)
some - one ___ like me.)

C   C/E   Fmaj7

(1.,2.) Oh, _____   oh. _____

(2.) Some-one __ like   me.

C   C/E

Oh, _____   oh. _____

Fmaj7   Am7

____   Some-one __ like   me.   Oh, _____ Some-bod - y.

C   Fmaj7

oh. _____

Am7

C

Fmaj7

Oh, _____ oh. _____

1

2

D

Off in the night, _____ I'm

F#m

read - y, I'm read - y, I'm read - y, I'm

D

F#m

read - y, I'm read - y, I'm read - y, I'm

read - y.   *Guitar solo*

Some - one __ like   you,

some - bod - y.

VIDEO

Words and Music by REGINALD HARGIS, CARLOS BROADY,
INDIA.ARIE and SHANNON SANDERS

Some-times I shave my legs___ and some-times I don't.

Some-times I comb my hair___ and some-times I won't.___ De-

*Vocal is written one octave higher than sung.

Bm7 Am7 Bm7 Em7

pend-ing how the wind blows, I might e - ven paint my toes. ___ It

Bm7 Am7 Bm7 Em7

real - ly just de-pends on what - ev - er feels good in my soul. ___ I'm

Bm7 Am7 Bm7

not the av - 'rage girl from your vid - e - o ___ and I ain't built like a

Em7 Bm7 Am7

su - per - mod - el, ___ but I learned to love my-self un - con - di - tion - al - ly be - cause ___

I am a queen. I'm not the av-'rage girl from your video, my worth is not de-ter-mined by the price of my clothes. No mat-ter what I'm wear-ing, I will al-ways be In-di-a A-rie.

When I look in the mir-ror and the on-ly one there is me,

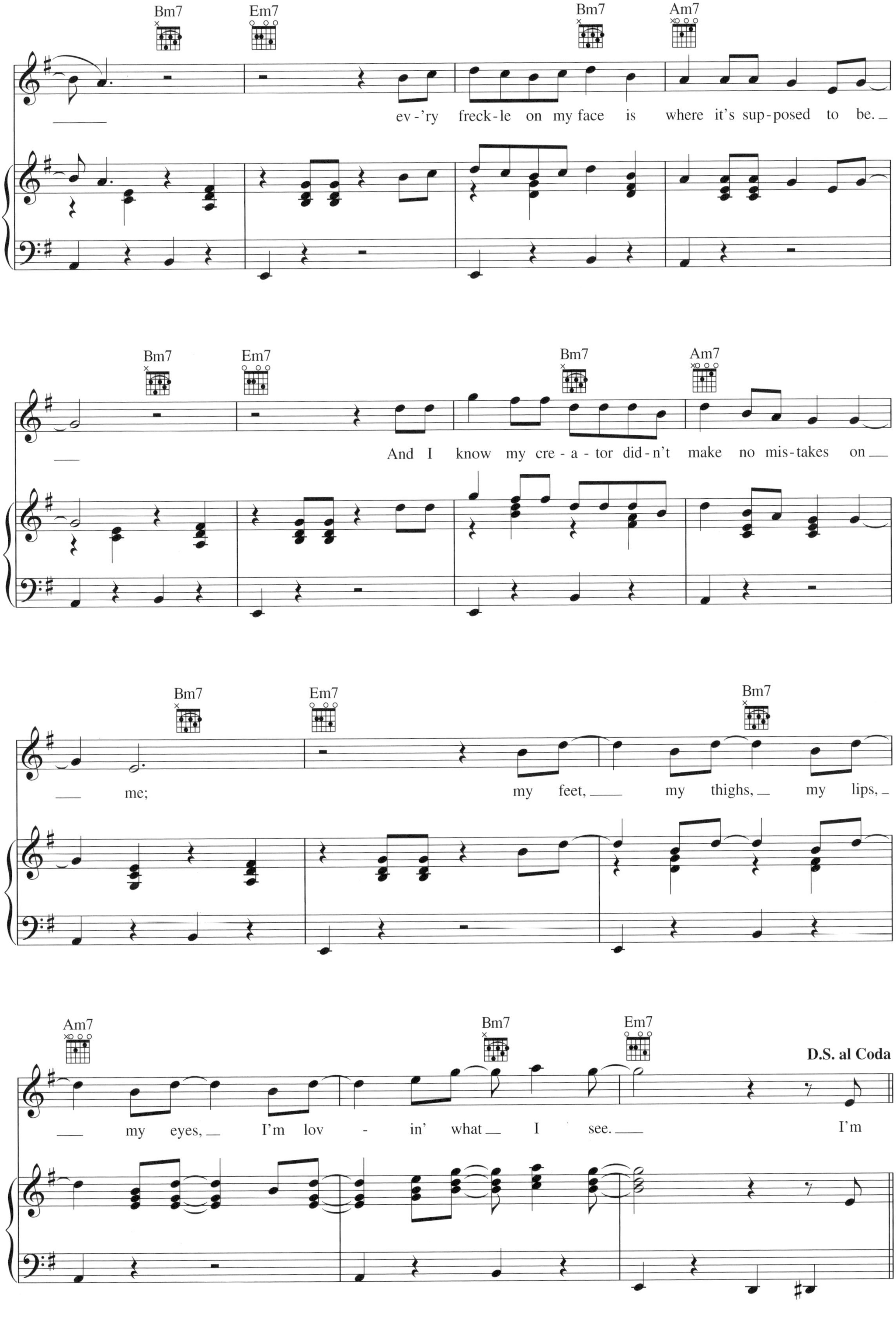

CODA

Em11 Cmaj7 Bm7 Am Em/G Am7

Am I less of a la-dy if I don't wear pan-ty-hose?

Cmaj7 Bm7 Am Em/G

My mom-ma said, "A la-dy ain't what she wears but what __ she knows." __

Am7 Cmaj7 Bm7 Am7 Em/G

But I've drawn the con-clu-sion, it's all an il-lu-sion; con-

Am7 Cmaj7 Bm7 Am7 G6/9

fu-sion's the name of the game. __ A mis-con-cep-tion, a vast de-cep-tion, some-thing's got-ta change.___ Don't be of-fend-ed; this is all my o-pin-ion. Ain't

noth-in' that I'm___ say-in' law.___ This is a true con-fes-sion of a life-learned les-son I was

sent here to share with y'all.___ So get in where you fit in, go on and shine;___

clear your mind,___ now's the time.__ Put your salt on the shelf,_ go on and love your-self,_'cause ev-'ry-thing's gon-na be al - right. I'm not the av-'rage girl from your vid - e - o ___ and

I ain't built like a su - per-mod - el, ___ but I learned to love my - self un - con -

di - tion - al - ly be - cause ___ I am ___ a queen. ___ I'm

not the av-'rage girl from your vid - e - o, ___ my worth is not de - ter-mined by the price of my clothes. _ No mat-ter what I'm wear-ing I will al - ways be ___ In -

- di - a ___ A - rie. ___ Keep your fan - cy drinks _ and your ex -

pen - sive minks, _ I don't need that to have a good time. Keep your ex -

pen - sive cars ___ and your cav - i - ar; ___ all's ___ I need ___ is my gui -

tar. Keep your Cris - tal and your pis - tol, I'd

rath - er have a pret - ty piece of crys - tal. Don't need your sil - i - cone, __ I pre -

fer my own; __ what God gave me is just fine. I'm

not the av -'rage girl from your vid - e - o ____ and I ain't built like a

WE BELONG TOGETHER

Words and Music by MARIAH CAREY,
JERMAINE DUPRI, MANUEL SEAL,
JOHNTA AUSTIN, DARNELL BRISTOL,
KENNETH EDMONDS, SIDNEY JOHNSON,
PATRICK MOTEN, BOBBY WOMACK
and SANDRA SULLY

Slow Soul

Ah, _____ oh, _____ sweet love. _

(Spoken:) Yeah.

I did-n't mean it when I

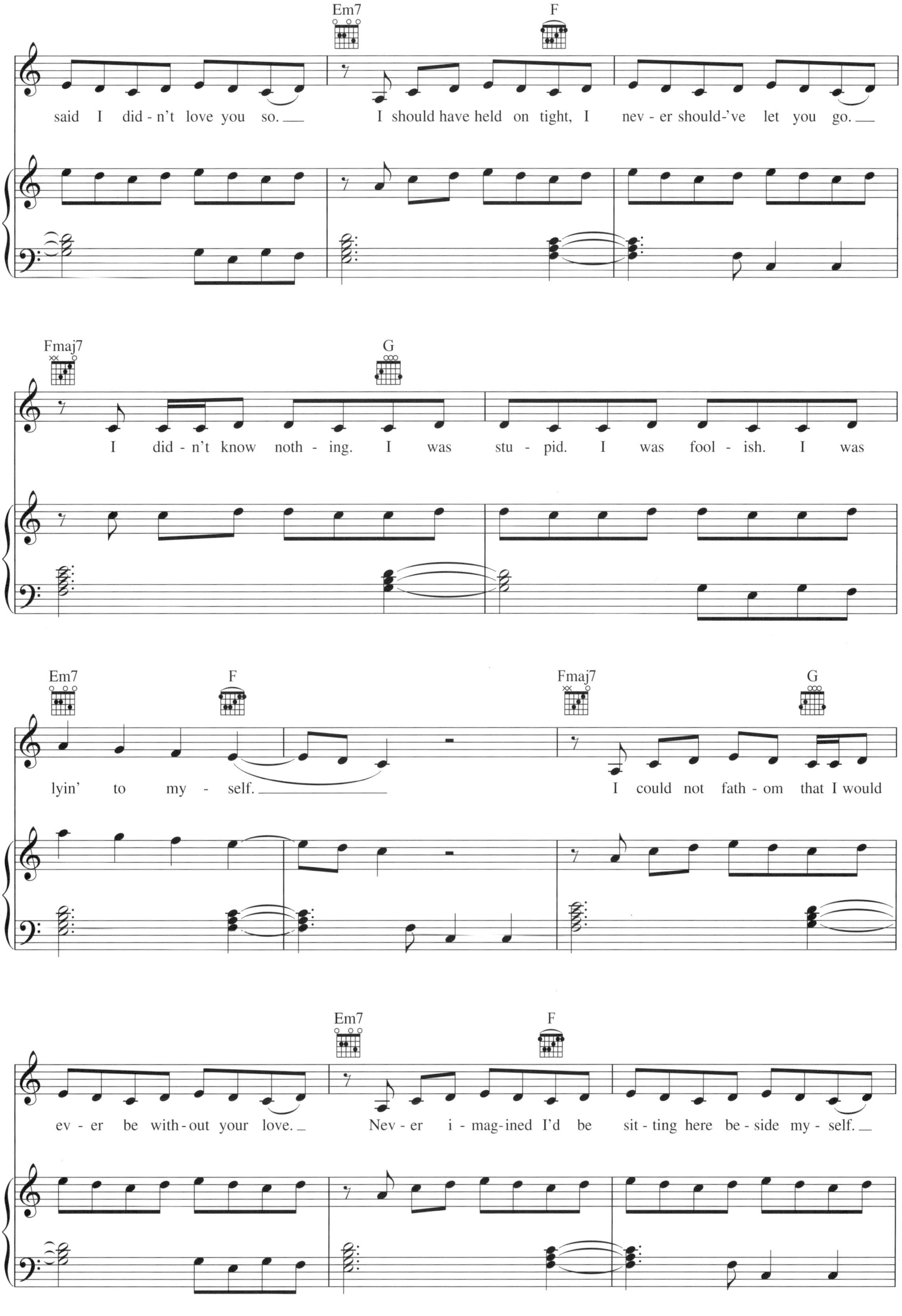

Guess I did-n't know you, guess I did-n't know me. But I thought I knew ev-'ry-thing.

I nev-er felt ____ the feel-ing that I'm feel-ing

now that I don't hear your voice or have your touch and kiss your lips 'cause I don't have a choice.

Oh, what I would-n't give to have you ly-ing by my side right here. 'Cause,

Fmaj7
G
ba - by, when you left I lost a part of
Em7
F
Fmaj7
G
me. It's still so hard to be - lieve. Come back,
Em7
F
ba - by, please, 'cause we be - long to - geth - er. Who else am I gon-na
Fmaj7
G
lean on when times get rough? Who's gon-na talk to

Em7 | **F**

me on the phone till the sun comes up? Who's __ gon-na take your

Fmaj7 | **G** | **To Coda** ⊕ | **Em7** | **F**

place? There ain't no-bod-y bet - ter. Oh ba-by, ba-by, we be-long __ to-geth -

Fmaj7 | **G**

er. I can't sleep at night __ when you are on my mind. _ Bob-by

Em7 | **F** | **Fmaj7** | **G**

Wo-mack's on the ra-di-o sing-in' to me, "If you think you're lone-ly

N.C.
now." Wait a min - ute, this is too deep, too deep. I got - ta change the sta - tion. So I
Fmaj7 G Em7 F
turn the dial, try - in' to catch a break. And then I hear Ba - by - face.
Fmaj7 G
"I on - ly think of you" and it's break - in' my heart. I'm try - in' to
Em7 F Fmaj7 G
keep it to - geth - er but I'm fall - ing a - part. I'm feel - ing all out of my el - e - ment.

Em7   F

Throw - ing things, cry - ing, try - in' to fig - ure out where the hell I went

Fmaj7   G

wrong. The pain re - flect - ed in this song ain't e - ven half of what I'm

Em7   F

feel - ing in - side.____ I need you, need you back in my life.____

D.S. al Coda

Ba - by,

CODA   Em7   F

we be - long ____ to - geth - er,

Fmaj7
G
ba - by. When you left I lost a part of
Em7
F
Fmaj7
G
me. It's still so hard to be - lieve. Come back,
Em7
F
ba - by, please, 'cause we be - long to - geth - er. Who am I gon - na
Fmaj7
G
lean on when times get rough? Who's gon - na talk to

me till the sun comes up? Who's gon-na take your

place? There ain't no-bod-y bet - er. Oh, ba-by, ba-by, we be-long __ to-geth -

er. Ooo, yeah. ____

Repeat and Fade **Optional Ending**

Ooo, yeah. ____

YOU BELONG WITH ME

Words and Music by TAYLOR SWIFT
and LIZ ROSE

Moderately fast

mf

You're on the phone with your girl-friend. She's up-set. ___

___ She's go-in' off a-bout some-thin' that ___ you said, ___ 'cause she does-n't

get your hu-mor like I do.

* *Recorded a half step lower.*

G

I'm in the room, it's a typ-i-cal Tues-day night. ___ I'm lis-t'nin' to the kind of

Am7

mu-sic she does-n't like. ___ And she'll nev-er know your sto - ry like

C

I do. But she wears short skirts,

Am7

She wears high heels,

C

I wear T - shirts.
I wear sneak - ers.

G

She's cheer cap-tain and

D

I'm on the bleach-ers,

dream-in' 'bout the day when you wake up and find __ that what you're look- in' for __ has been here __

__ the whole time. If you could see that I'm __ the one __ who un-der-stands you.

Been here all __ a - long. __ So why can't you see __

To Coda

__ you be - long __ with me? _____ You be - long __ with me. __

Walk - in' the streets with you __ in your worn - out jeans, __ I can't help think - in' this is how it ought __ to be. __

Laugh - in' on a park bench, think - in' to my - self, __ "Hey, is - n't this eas __ - y?" __ And you've got a smile that could light up this __ whole town. __

I have-n't seen it in a while since she brought you down. You say you're fine. I know you

bet- ter than that. Hey, what you do- in' with a girl like that?

D.S. al Coda

CODA

me? Stand - in' by ___ and wait-

- in' at your back door. All this time ___ how could ___ you not know, ba - by, ___ you be - long __ with me? _____ You be - long __ with me. __

Oh, I re - mem - ber you driv - in' to my house in the

C   G

mid - dle of the night. I'm the one who makes you laugh when you

D   Am7

know you're 'bout to cry. I know your fav - 'rite songs and you

C   G

tell me 'bout your dreams. Think I know where you be - long. Think I

D   G

know it's with me. _____ Can't you see that I'm ___ the one ___ who un-der-stands you? Been here all ___ a - long. ___ So why can't you

see ___ you be-long ___ with me? ___

___ Stand - in' by ___ here, wait - in' at your back door.

All this time ___ how could ___ you not know, ba - by, ___

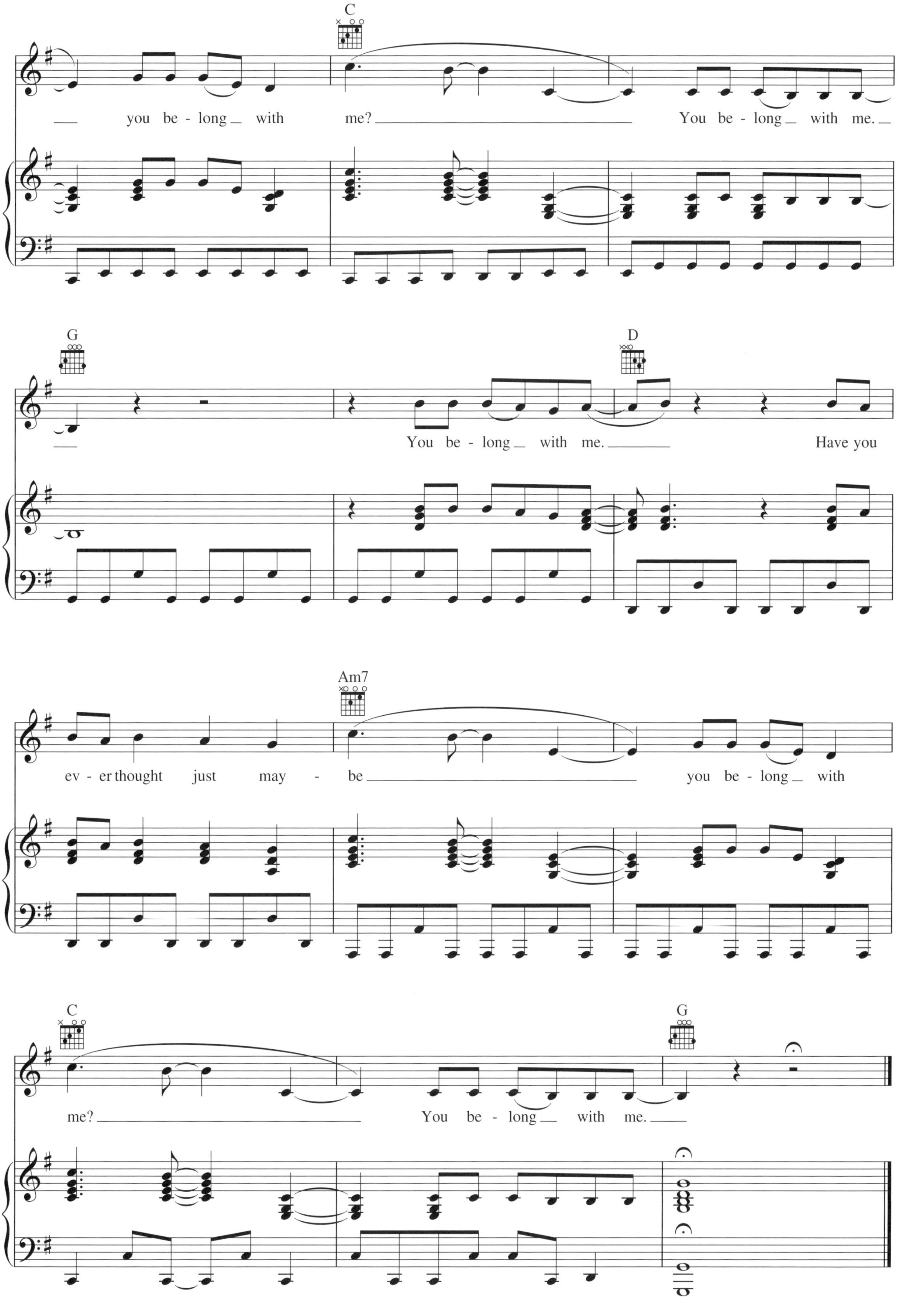

WHERE WERE YOU
(When the World Stopped Turning)

Words and Music by
ALAN JACKSON

Moderately fast

Where were you when the world ___ stopped turn-in' that Sep - tem - ber

day? Out in the yard ___ with your wife and chil - dren or
Teach-in' a class ___ full of in - no - cent chil - dren or

G
C
F
work - in' on some stage _ in L. A.? Did you stand there in shock at the
driv - in' on some cold _ in - ter - state? Did you feel guilt - y 'cause _
C
F
C
sight of that black smoke ris - in' a - gainst that blue sky? Did you
you're a sur - viv - or, in a crowd - ed room did you feel a - lone? Did you
F
C
Am
shout out in an - ger in fear for your neigh - bor, or did you just sit down and
call up your moth - er and tell her you love her? Did you dust off that Bi - ble at
F
G
C
cry? Did you weep for the chil - dren, they
home? Did you o - pen your eyes and hope

G

lost their dear loved ones, pray for the ones ___ who don't know?
it nev - er hap - pened, close your eyes and not go to sleep?

C

Did you re -
Did you

3

joice for the peo - ple who walked from the rub - ble and sob for the ones ___ left be -
no - tice the sun - set for the first time in ag - es and speak to some stran - ger on the

G

C

low?
street?

Did you burst out in pride for the Red, White and Blue ___ and
Did you lay down at night and ___ think of to - mor - row,

F

3

C

F

C

F

he - roes who died just do - in' what they do?
go out and buy you a gun?

Did you look up to heav - en for
Did you turn off that vio - lent old

some kind __ of an - swer and look at your - self __ and what real - ly mat - ters?
mov - ie _____ you're watch - in' and

I'm just a sing - er of __ sim - ple songs. I'm not a

real po - lit - i - cal __ man. I watch C - N - N, ___ but I'm not __

___ sure I can tell you the dif - f'rence in I - raq and I - ran. But

I know Je - sus and I _____ talk to God _____ and I re - mem - ber this from when I was

young: faith, hope and love are some good things He gave us

and the great - est is love.

D.S. al Coda

CODA

turn on "I Love Lu - cy" re - runs? Did you go to a church _____ and hold

C F C
hands with some stran - ger, stand in line to give your own blood? Did you
F C Am
just stay home and cling tight to your fam-'ly, thank God you have some-bod - y to love?
F F
I'm just a sing - er of
C F C
sim - ple songs. I'm not a real po - lit - i - cal man. I watch

C - N - N, ___ but I'm not ___ sure I can tell you the dif-f'rence in I - raq and I -

ran. But I know Je - sus and I ___ talk to God ___ and I re -

mem - ber this from when I was young: faith, hope and love are some

good things He gave us and the great - est is love.

love,

and the great - est is love,

and the great - est is love.

Where were you when the world _____ stopped turn - in'

that Sep - tem - ber day? _____

YOU'RE BEAUTIFUL

Words and Music by JAMES BLUNT,
SACHA SCARBECK and AMANDA GHOST

Moderately slow

My life is bril - liant.

My life is bril - liant, my love is pure.

I saw an an - gel, of that I'm sure. ___ She smiled

at me on the sub - way, she was with an - oth - er man. ___ But I ___

___ won't lose no sleep all night, ___ 'cos I've ___ got a plan. ___

(1.,2.) You're beau-ti - ful. ___ You're beau-ti - ful. ___
(3.) You're beau-ti - ful. ___ You're beau-ti - ful. ___

You're beau-ti - ful, ___ it's true. ___ I saw ___ your face ___ in a
You're beau-ti - ful, ___ it's true. ___ There must ___ be an an-gel ___ with a

crowd - ed ___ place. ___ And I don't know what ___ to ___ do,
smile on her face ___ when she

___ 'cos I'll nev - er ___ be ___ with you. ___

Yes, she caught my eye as I walked on by. She could see from my face that I was fuck-ing high. And I don't think that I'll see her a-gain, but we shared a mo-ment that will last till the end.

D.S. al Coda I

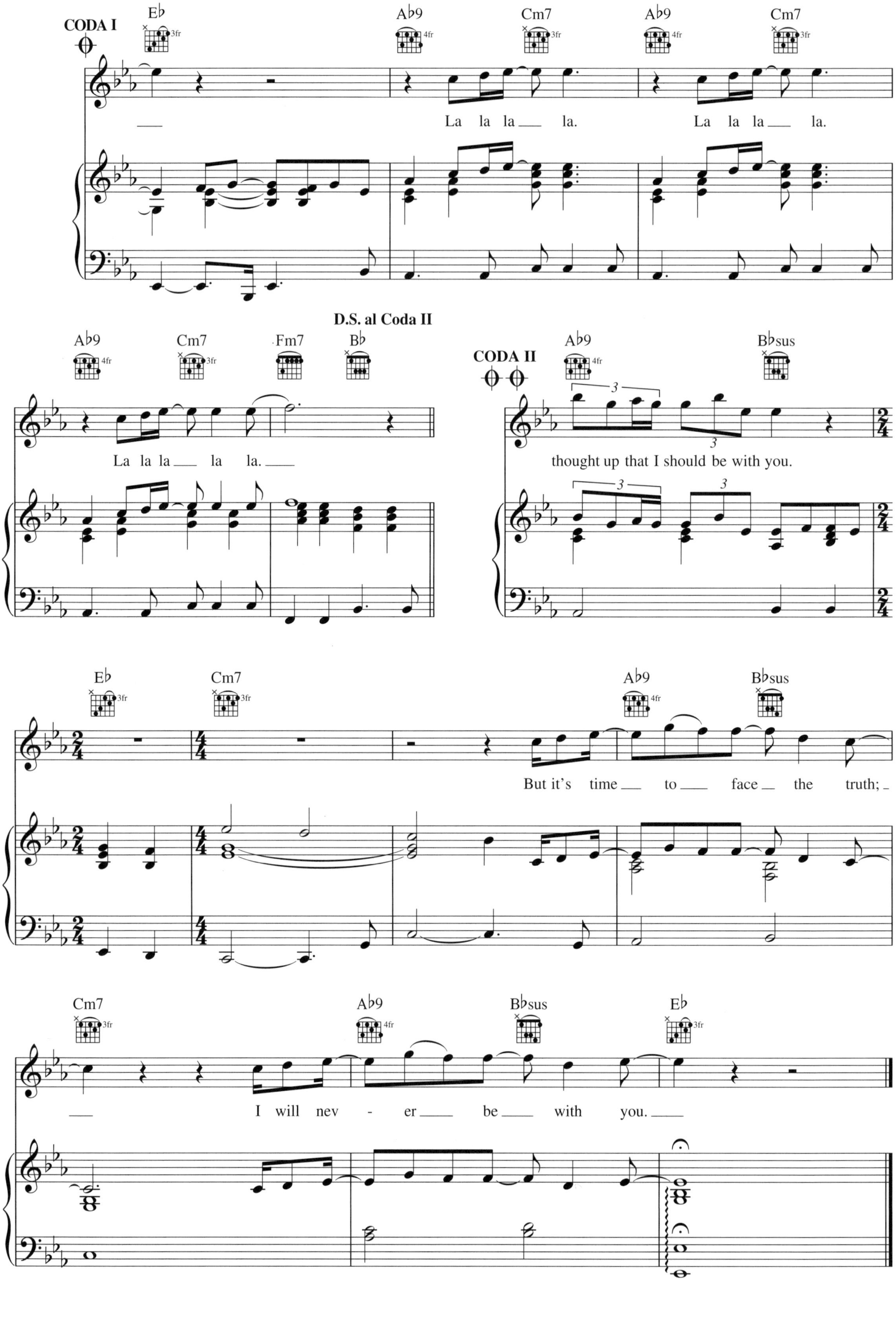

THE GRAMMY AWARDS®
SONGBOOKS FROM HAL LEONARD

These elite collections of the nominees and winners of
Grammy Awards since the honor's inception in 1958
provide a snapshot of the changing times in popular music.

PIANO/VOCAL/GUITAR

GRAMMY AWARDS RECORD OF THE YEAR 1958-2011

Beat It • Beautiful Day • Bridge over Troubled Water • Don't Know Why • Don't Worry, Be Happy • The Girl from Ipanema (Garôta De Ipanema) • Hotel California • I Will Always Love You • Just the Way You Are • Mack the Knife • Moon River • My Heart Will Go on (Love Theme from 'Titanic') • Rehab • Sailing • Unforgettable • Up, Up and Away • The Wind Beneath My Wings • and more.
00313603 P/V/G........................$16.99

THE GRAMMY AWARDS SONG OF THE YEAR 1958-1969

Battle of New Orleans • Born Free • Fever • The Good Life • A Hard Day's Night • Harper Valley P.T.A. • Hello, Dolly! • Hey Jude • King of the Road • Little Green Apples • Mrs. Robinson • Ode to Billy Joe • People • Somewhere, My Love • Strangers in the Night • A Time for Us (Love Theme) • Volare • Witchcraft • Yesterday • and more.
00313598 P/V/G........................$16.99

THE GRAMMY AWARDS SONG OF THE YEAR 1970-1979

Alone Again (Naturally) • American Pie • At Seventeen • Don't It Make My Brown Eyes Blue • Honesty • (I Never Promised You A) Rose Garden • I Write the Songs • Killing Me Softly with His Song • Let It Be • Me and Bobby McGee • Send in the Clowns • Song Sung Blue • Stayin' Alive • Three Times a Lady • The Way We Were • You're So Vain • You've Got a Friend • and more.
00313599 P/V/G........................$16.99

THE GRAMMY AWARDS SONG OF THE YEAR 1980-1989

Against All Odds (Take a Look at Me Now) • Always on My Mind • Beat It • Bette Davis Eyes • Don't Worry, Be Happy • Ebony and Ivory • Endless Love • Every Breath You Take • Eye of the Tiger • Fame • Fast Car • Hello • I Just Called to Say I Love You • La Bamba • Nine to Five • The Rose • Somewhere Out There • Time After Time • We Are the World • and more.
00313600 P/V/G........................$16.99

THE GRAMMY AWARDS SONG OF THE YEAR 1990-1999

Can You Feel the Love Tonight • (Everything I Do) I Do It for You • From a Distance • Give Me One Reason • I Swear • Kiss from a Rose • Losing My Religion • My Heart Will Go on (Love Theme from 'Titanic') • Nothing Compares 2 U • Smooth • Streets of Philadelphia • Tears in Heaven • Unforgettable • Walking in Memphis • A Whole New World • You Oughta Know • and more.
00313601 P/V/G........................$16.99

THE GRAMMY AWARDS SONG OF THE YEAR 2000-2009

Beautiful • Beautiful Day • Breathe • Chasing Pavements • Complicated • Dance with My Father • Daughters • Don't Know Why • Fallin' • I Hope You Dance • I'm Yours • Live like You Were Dying • Poker Face • Rehab • Single Ladies (Put a Ring on It) • A Thousand Miles • Umbrella • Use Somebody • Viva La Vida • and more.
00313602 P/V/G........................$16.99

THE GRAMMY AWARDS BEST COUNTRY SONG 1964-2011

Always on My Mind • Before He Cheats • Behind Closed Doors • Bless the Broken Road • Butterfly Kisses • Dang Me • Forever and Ever, Amen • The Gambler • I Still Believe in You • I Swear • King of the Road • Live like You Were Dying • Love Can Build a Bridge • Need You Now • On the Road Again • White Horse • You Decorated My Life • and more.
00313604 P/V/G........................$16.99

THE GRAMMY AWARDS BEST R&B SONG 1958-2011

After the Love Has Gone • Ain't No Sunshine • Be Without You • Billie Jean • End of the Road • Good Golly Miss Molly • Hit the Road Jack • If You Don't Know Me by Now • Papa's Got a Brand New Bag • Respect • Shine • Single Ladies (Put a Ring on It) • (Sittin' On) the Dock of the Bay • Superstition • U Can't Touch This • We Belong Together • and more.
00313605 P/V/G........................$16.99

THE GRAMMY AWARDS BEST POP & ROCK GOSPEL ALBUMS (2000-2011)

Call My Name • Come on Back to Me • Deeper Walk • Forever • Gone • I Need You • I Smile • I Will Follow • King • Leaving 99 • Lifesong • Looking Back at You • Much of You • My Love Remains • Say So • Somebody's Watching • Step by Step/Forever We Will Sing • Tunnel • Unforgetful You • You Hold My World • Your Love Is a Song • and more.
00313680 P/V/G........................$16.99

ELECTRONIC KEYBOARD

THE GRAMMY AWARDS RECORD OF THE YEAR 1958-2011 – VOL. 160

All I Wanna Do • Bridge over Troubled Water • Don't Know Why • The Girl from Ipanema (Garôta De Ipanema) • Hotel California • I Will Always Love You • Just the Way You Are • Killing Me Softly with His Song • Love Will Keep Us Together • Rehab • Unforgettable • What's Love Got to Do with It • The Wind Beneath My Wings • and more.
00100315 E-Z Play Today #160.....................$16.99

PRO VOCAL
WOMEN'S EDITIONS

THE GRAMMY AWARDS BEST FEMALE POP VOCAL PERFORMANCE 1990-1999 — VOL. 57

Book/CD Pack

All I Wanna Do • Building a Mystery • Constant Craving • I Will Always Love You • I Will Remember You • My Heart Will Go on (Love Theme from 'Titanic') • No More "I Love You's" • Something to Talk About (Let's Give Them Something to Talk About) • Unbreak My Heart • Vision of Love.
00740446 Melody/Lyrics/Chords.................$14.99

THE GRAMMY AWARDS BEST FEMALE POP VOCAL PERFORMANCE 2000-2009 – VOL. 58

Book/CD Pack

Ain't No Other Man • Beautiful • Chasing Pavements • Don't Know Why • Halo • I Try • I'm like a Bird • Rehab • Since U Been Gone • Sunrise.
00740447 Melody/Lyrics/Chords.................$14.99

MEN'S EDITIONS

THE GRAMMY AWARDS BEST MALE POP VOCAL PERFORMANCE 1990-1999 – VOL. 59

Book/CD Pack

Brand New Day • Can You Feel the Love Tonight • Candle in the Wind 1997 • Change the World • If I Ever Lose My Faith in You • Kiss from a Rose • My Father's Eyes • Oh, Pretty Woman • Tears in Heaven • When a Man Loves a Woman.
00740448 Melody/Lyrics/Chords.................$14.99

THE GRAMMY AWARDS BEST MALE POP VOCAL PERFORMANCE 2000-2009 – VOL. 60

Book/CD Pack

Cry Me a River • Daughters • Don't Let Me Be Lonely Tonight • Make It Mine • Say • Waiting on the World to Change • What Goes Around...Comes Around Interlude • Your Body Is a Wonderland.
00740449 Melody/Lyrics/Chords.................$14.99

Prices, contents, and availabilbility subject to change without notice.

HAL•LEONARD® CORPORATION

7777 W. BLUEMOUND RD. P.O. BOX 13819 MILWAUKEE, WI 53213

www.halleonard.com